P9-DJV-946

KID
ATHLETES
TRUE TALES OF CHILDHOOD FROM
SPORTS LEGENDS
STORIES BY DAVID STABLER ILLUSTRATIONS BY DOOGIE HORNER

Library of Congress Cataloging in
Publication Number: 2014956803

ISBN: 978-1-59474-802-8

Printed in China
Typeset in Vitesse, Forza, and Branboll

Designed by Andie Reid based on a design by Doogie Horner
Illustrations by Doogie Horner
Illustration coloring by Mario Zucca
Production management by John J. McGurk

Quirk Books
215 Church Street
Philadelphia, PA 19106
quirkbooks.com

10 9 8 7 6

KID ATHLETES

TRUE TALES OF CHILDHOOD FROM

SPORTS LEGENDS

STORIES BY *DAVID STABLER* ILLUSTRATIONS BY *DOOGIE HORNER*

TABLE OF CONTENTS

PART TWO

FAMILY MATTERS

PART THREE

PRACTICE MAKES PERFECT

★ INTRODUCTION ★

You may have heard their names. You may have seen their highlights. Maybe you've even cheered for them from the bleachers. The superstar athletes profiled in this book are world famous for their remarkable achievements. But we bet there's a lot about them that you don't know.

For example, did you know that NFL quarterback Peyton Manning once dared to dance the tango in front of his entire middle school?

Or that race car driver Danica Patrick got her start pushing the pedals on a go-kart?

Or that legendary hockey player Bobby Orr grew up picking worms on a farm?

Long before they became sports champions, these future superstars were just little kids who liked to run, jump, and play like everyone else.

Some of them learned early on that they had a special talent and then practiced every day to make sure they became the best they could be at their chosen sport.

Others had to leap over obstacles on the road to fame and fortune. Before they ever defeated an opponent on the playing field, boxing ring, basketball court, or racetrack, they had to figure out how to overcome the special challenges that threatened to hold them back.

Before vaulting to Olympic gold, gymnast Gabby Douglas first had to learn how to deal with bullies.

Basketball player Yao Ming grew up thinking that he was too tall to fit through a doorway—let alone make it in the professional basketball leagues of the NBA.

Lionel Messi had the opposite problem. One day, he would become the world's biggest soccer star. But as a kid, he was told many times that he was too small to succeed on the team.

And all these great athletes—no matter where or when they lived—had homework to finish, parents to answer to, and brothers and sisters to deal with. Not to mention the occasional unruly horse.

In *Kid Athletes*, we'll ride along with the superheroes of sports and learn how they began their charge into the record books. Each took a different path to get there. But they all had one thing in common:

Every one of these amazing athletes started out as a little kid.

Part ONE

It's Not Easy Being a Kid

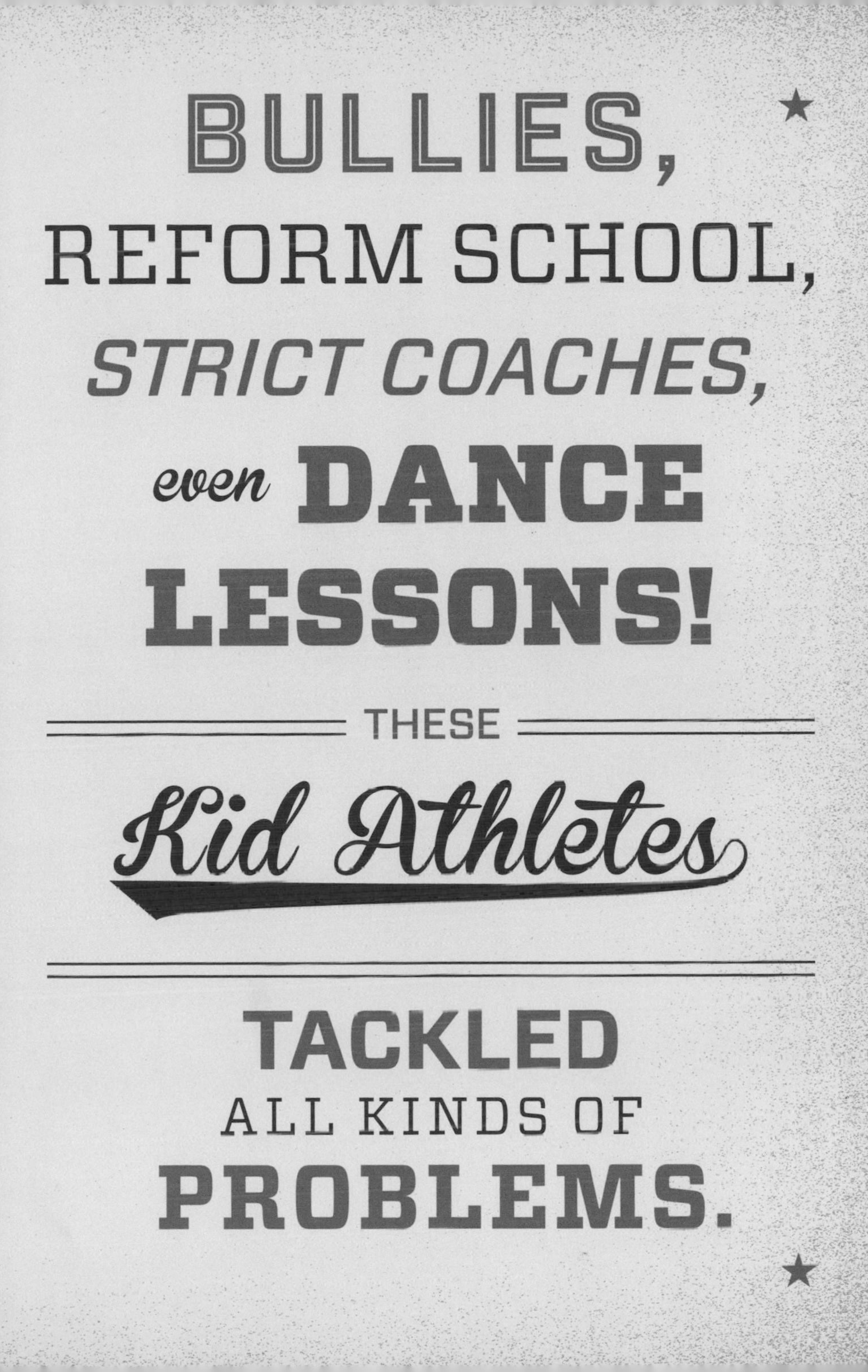
BULLIES,
REFORM SCHOOL,
STRICT COACHES,
even DANCE
LESSONS!
THESE
Kid Athletes
TACKLED
ALL KINDS OF
PROBLEMS.

BABE RUTH

Bad Boy Makes Good

Not all great athletes are born great. In fact, some of them start out downright bad. Babe Ruth went from being a wild, unruly kid roaming the streets of Baltimore to reigning as baseball's home-run king—all thanks to the guidance of a kindly "big brother" who took him under his wing.

"I was a bad kid," admitted Babe Ruth in his autobiography. Like many things the loud and boisterous New York Yankees legend said, that was something of an understatement.

In fact, "Little George," as he was known before he earned his famous nickname, was officially labeled "incorrigible" by his own parents. He was impossible to control at the age of eight!

How did little George get so bad? For starters, he learned about misbehaving right under his own roof. On the ground floor of the Ruth family's apartment was the roughest, toughest saloon in the city of Baltimore. It was run by his father, Big George. The crowd was rowdy, the whiskey was cheap, and the patrons were constantly quarrelsome.

Little George's parents worked twenty hours a day. That left George on his own a lot. He almost never went to school. "I was a bum when I was a kid," he said as an adult. He roamed the streets of the teeming city looking for trouble. More often than not, he found it.

Little George stole fruit from the stands that lined the sidewalks. He threw eggs and rotten apples at the carriage drivers as they passed. His parents grew more and more frustrated with his rabble-rousing ways.

No one is sure exactly when, or why, Little George's parents decided they could no longer care for their son. It's possible that they had to send him away because of a terrible brawl in the saloon. Gunshots were fired; the police were called. A neighbor told the officers, "A little kid is living in there. That's no place for a child." Or perhaps George's mom just got fed up with her son playing hooky and causing trouble.

So when Little George was seven, his parents asked a local official to declare him incorrigible and send him to a reformatory. On Friday the thirteenth of June in 1902, Big George dropped off his son at his new home: St. Mary's Industrial School for Orphans, Delinquent, Incorrigible, and Wayward Boys.

The school was as grim as its name. Eight hundred orphans, runaways, and unruly boys were packed into six identical gray buildings surrounded by an impenetrable fence. A set of imposing iron gates kept the boys in and everyone else out. Thirty members of a religious order—called Xaverian brothers—were in charge of feeding, clothing, teaching, and disciplining the boys, who ranged in age from seven to twenty-one. Little George was one of the youngest residents.

When he learned that he would have to stay there for the next thirteen years, Little George burst into tears. He would miss being able to do whatever he wanted. But he had no choice. In those days, reform school was considered the only way to make a bad boy good again. His father left him in the hands of the brothers and hoped for the best.

Little George was shown to a stark room in a dormitory that housed two hundred other students. All the boys wore a uniform of jackets and ties. Each one was issued a small blackboard and a pencil to record schoolwork. Students used their jacket sleeves to wipe the slates clean at the end of the day.

George quickly learned the school routine. Every day, a bell woke everyone up at 6 a.m. sharp. Talking was forbidden during meals, which consisted mostly of soup and bread. On Sundays the boys might get one or two hot dogs or slices of baloney. Bedtime was at 8 p.m. A night watchman kept an eye on the boys until morning. Sometimes, if the watchman was sick and unable to work, one of the boys was asked to fill in. In return, the boy was given an extra-large breakfast the next morning. Each boy was also given a job. George's job was to stitch collars onto shirts.

He worked five and a half days a week and had Sundays off. Most students spent their free day playing baseball in the schoolyard. Despite his nickname, Little George was already a big, strapping kid, and he enjoyed the recreation part of the reform school routine most of all.

Although he wasn't happy with all the rules and restrictions, Little George got along well with his classmates at St. Mary's. Sometimes he used the money he earned to buy candy for the boys who couldn't afford it. He even tried to help some of the smaller kids. One day, a boy named Loads Clark confessed that he had accidentally broken a window in a school building. So George offered to take the blame.

Little George earned the respect of his reform-school classmates, but still he was often lonely and sad. Visiting Day was the worst. On one such occasion when his friend Lou "Fats" Leisman found him sitting all alone, George told him unhappily, "I guess I am too big and ugly for anyone to come to see me."

Eventually, one of the Xaverian brothers noticed how unhappy Little George was, and he decided to help. Brother Matthias was prefect of discipline at St. Mary's. His job was to dole out punishment and work to help the most incorrigible kids at school—and no one was more incorrigible than Little George.

Everyone at St. Mary's was in awe of Brother Matthias. Standing six foot six inches tall and weighing nearly three hundred pounds, the stern disciplinarian looked like a giant. Rumor had it that he needed an extra-long bed to sleep in, and that he hung his bedroom door on the outside of the door jamb to give himself more room to pass through. The boys had a special nickname for him:

Despite his imposing size, Brother Matthias was a mild-mannered man who seldom raised his voice. He didn't have to. One day, when a fight broke out in the schoolyard, Matthias rushed out to the site of the problem. As soon as the squabbling kids saw "The Boss," a hush fell over them and they quickly dispersed.

When he wasn't keeping the peace, Brother Matthias liked to teach a master class in his favorite subject: baseball. On Sunday evenings after supper, he would gather the boys in the schoolyard and put on an exhibition of batting prowess the likes of which none of them had ever seen. With his special fungo bat in one hand and a hardball in the other, Brother Matthias would swat a series of high-arcing moonshots.

Among the boys clambering to retrieve the balls was Little George, who saw in the burly brother a perfect role model for what *he* could do if he set his mind to it.

One day, Matthias invited George to throw around a ball for a while. Soon they were playing catch every day. Almost without realizing it, George began to imitate Brother Matthias's walk as well as his epic swing.

When George improved, Matthias invited him to join the school's baseball team. Little George was thrilled. "What position will I play?"

When George tried on the catcher's mitt, he noticed a slight problem. He was left-handed, and the mitt was made for a righty. But George didn't let that stop him. With a bit of practice, he developed a knack for catching the ball with his left hand, flipping it into the air while discarding the mitt, and then plucking the ball out of the air in time to throw it. Tricks like that, along with his powerful swing, made him one of the team's standout players.

Brother Matthias didn't just teach Little George about baseball. He also kept him from falling back into his old bad habits. Once when he caught George laughing at the team's pitcher for having a tough game, he decided to teach his charge a lesson.

Signaling to the umpire for a timeout, Matthias handed the ball to George, who had never pitched before. Little George wasn't laughing anymore. But he concentrated on the task and allowed no hits for the rest of the game. He became one of the team's best pitchers—and learned about compassion and sportsmanship as well.

George had a new sense of belonging, but he still didn't like reform school. He once ran away from St. Mary's and spent three days on the lam before authorities tracked him down. On his return, Brother Matthias issued the worst punishment possible: no baseball.

After standing alone outside the schoolyard, George was filled with remorse. With the lesson learned, Brother Matthias welcomed George back to the team and allowed him to play again.

George's teammates were happy to have him back, but they knew he wouldn't be with them for long. With each passing year, George was growing bigger and stronger and outperforming his opponents. He clouted more than sixty home runs in a single season. When he first started playing baseball at age nine, George was pitted against twelve-year-olds. By the time he was sixteen, he was matched with players as old as twenty. Newspapers began to publish stories about the reform-school kid with the amazing home-run swing.

Brother Matthias knew it was time for George to move on, so he arranged for tryouts with local semi-professional teams. In 1914, the owner of the Baltimore Orioles, Jack Dunn, visited St Mary's. Brother Matthias told him all about George's hitting and pitching prowess. Dunn was so impressed that he offered the nineteen-year-old a contract on the spot.

A few weeks later, Jack Dunn returned to St. Mary's to pick up his new rookie. Brother Matthias escorted George to the iron gate and said goodbye. George shook his hand and thanked Matthias for all he had done for him. "You'll make it, George," Brother Matthias said. And with that, George loaded his suitcase into Dunn's red car and left for North Carolina, where he joined the Orioles at their spring training camp.

That was the beginning of Babe Ruth's rise to fame. But it was not the end of his friendship with Brother Matthias. In 1919, a fire destroyed most of St. Mary's Industrial School.

Little George, now the Major League Baseball star known as Babe Ruth, volunteered to raise money to help the school. He invited St. Mary's band to travel with his team, the New York Yankees, on their final road trip of the 1920 season. Temporarily renamed "Babe Ruth's Boys Band," they played concerts before ballgames and afterward collected donations from fans. With Babe's help, Brother Matthias and the Xaverian brothers were able to rebuild most of the buildings lost in the fire.

Years later, Babe Ruth's wife, Claire, explained why her husband had gone out of his way to help the man who had taken him under his wing.

"When Babe Ruth was twenty-three, the world loved him," she said. "When he was thirteen, only Brother Matthias loved him."

JACKIE ROBINSON

The Pride of Pepper Street

The first black player to make it to the Major Leagues, Jackie Robinson changed baseball—and America—forever. But before he made that historic leap, Jackie first had to choose between being the leader of his neighborhood gang or becoming a leader in his community.

Long before he completed the journey to the big leagues, Jackie Robinson made his own personal journey —cross-country from Cairo, Georgia, where he was born, to a new home in Pasadena, California.

The family had to move because when Jackie was just six months old, his father left for Texas to visit a brother. He did not return, and Jackie never saw him again. Jackie's mother, Mallie, was left to raise her five children alone. She moved the family to Pasadena to be closer to her brother and found work as a maid.

Mallie couldn't afford to pay someone to look after little Jackie during the day. So, every morning, his older sister Willa Mae took him to her kindergarten. Before the school bell rang, she'd sit him in the sandbox and kept an eye on him from her desk near the window until class was dismissed.

After a year, Jackie was old enough to go to school on his own. He began playing sports and quickly gained a reputation as one of the best athletes in town. Other kids would offer to share their lunches if Jackie agreed to play on their team.

Eventually, Jackie's mother moved the family out of their cramped apartment and into a house on Pepper Street. The Robinsons were the first black family on the street at a time when African Americans were subjected to discrimination because of the color of their skin. They were forbidden from using the town swimming pool except one day a week. They had to sit in the back of the local movie theater. Many grocery stores refused to sell fruits and vegetables to anyone who wasn't white.

Jackie's new neighbors didn't make things easy for his family. Some even signed a petition to force the Robinsons to move out.

Jackie grew so angry about the discrimination that he formed his own gang—it was made up of kids from African American, Mexican American, and Japanese American families. They called themselves the Pepper Street Gang.

The gang members took out their frustrations on the residents of Pasadena. They threw dirt bombs at passing cars, chased rabbits across the football field at the Rose Bowl, and stole fruit off sidewalk carts. They became a nuisance.

When they were really bored, the gang would lurk along the outskirts of the local country club and swipe stray balls hit by the golfers. When the coast was clear, the boys would gather all the balls and try to sell them back to the golfers.

The boys in the Pepper Street Gang looked up to Jackie because he was quick enough to dash out onto the fairway, grab a ball, and dart behind the bushes before anyone could catch him. And he was small enough to hide inside a storm drain to escape an angry golfer trying to track him down.

At last, one of Jackie's intended victims caught on to the swindle. "I'll make you a deal," he said when Jackie offered to sell him back his own golf ball. "Let's finish out the hole together. If I win, you give me back my ball. If you win, you get to keep the ball *and* I'll give you an extra dollar." The man handed Jackie a putter, and he accepted the man's challenge. Jackie ended up winning the hole and, with it, the wager.

Some of the Pepper Street Gang's antics were harmless, but other times they found themselves in serious trouble. The Pasadena police started following Jackie and his gang. Fortunately, the cops weren't the only ones keeping a close eye on Jackie. One day, the town's new pastor, a 25-year-old minister named Karl Downs, dropped by the gang's hangout and asked to see him.

Jackie was standing in the middle of the crowd, but he was too timid to step forward.

"Tell Jackie I want to see him at junior church," the reverend told the boys. And then he left.

Jackie went to the church and met Reverend Downs. To his surprise, the reverend didn't ask him to break up the gang. Instead, he proposed putting the boys to work building a new youth center for the church. He also invited Jackie and his friends to his house and let them have full access to his refrigerator.

Jackie agreed to help out. And that one decision ended up changing his life forever. Instead of taking out his anger on local shopkeepers and passing motorists,

Jackie channeled all his energy into making a positive difference in his community. He not only helped build the youth center, he also volunteered as a Sunday school teacher at Reverend Downs's church. During the week, he focused his attention away from gang activities and back to his studies and sports.

With the support of Reverend Downs, Jackie was able to graduate from high school and then move on to Pasadena Junior College. While there, he broke records in four different sports: baseball, basketball, track, and football. On the same Rose Bowl field where the Pepper Street Gang used to chase rabbits, Jackie returned a kickoff 104 yards for a touchdown.

Over the years, Jackie continued to rely on Reverend Downs for advice and inspiration. Sometimes, on Sunday mornings, after playing football on Saturday, Jackie would be tempted to sleep in. "But no matter how terrible I felt, I had to get up," he said. "It was impossible to shirk duty when Karl Downs was involved."

After college, Jackie was drafted into the U.S. Army, where, once again, he encountered discrimination. On weekends, he would often visit with Reverend Downs to talk about his troubles. When Jackie left the army, Reverend Downs hired him to coach sports at the small Texas college where he was serving as president. While there, Jackie accepted an offer to play for the Kansas City Monarchs, a baseball team in the Negro Leagues. And so began his journey into the history books.

On April 15, 1947, Jackie became the first African American to play in a Major League Baseball game.

He again had to endure taunts and bullying—this time from white players who resented having to share the field with a black player. But he persevered and ended up being named rookie of the year. That fall, Reverend Downs traveled to New York to watch Jackie play in his first World Series.

Jackie Robinson would play five more times in the World Series over his ten-year major league career. In 1962, he was elected to the Baseball Hall of Fame. Historians have praised him for refusing to fight back in the face of racial discrimination. But Jackie did fight back, in his own way, by being the best person he could be, instead of following the bad example of his enemies. That was a lesson he had learned from his days as the tiny terror of the Pepper Street Gang.

BILLIE JEAN KING

The Girl Who Ran on Racket Power

Before Billie Jean King, tennis was a sport played by wealthy women in frilly white dresses. She made it possible for anyone, from any background, to dream of one day winning the U.S. Open or Wimbledon championship. Like most pioneers, Billie Jean had to overcome obstacles on the road to greatness. This is the story of a girl who found a way to make it on talent alone.

Even as a kid growing up in Long Beach, California, Billie Jean Moffitt knew she was going places.

On the wall of her elementary school classroom hung a big map. During free periods, Billie Jean would walk over, pick a city, and point to it.

Back then, those destinations seemed far out of reach. Billie Jean's parents could not afford to take her to the cities she longed to visit. Her family did not have much extra money and was rarely able to travel beyond their hometown.

No one would have guessed that Billie Jean would become one of the greatest tennis players in the world, or that she would indeed visit many of the places she'd marked on the map.

When she was a kid, Billie Jean used to visit her father, a firefighter, and play at the firehouse.

Fighting fires was an important job, but it didn't pay a lot. Billie Jean's dad wore the same two pairs of shoes for eight years so he could afford to buy things for her and her brother Randy. Her mother hosted Tupperware parties and worked as an "Avon lady" selling beauty products to bring in extra money. But no matter how hard her parents tried, they still had trouble making ends meet and paying all their bills.

To make matters worse, the kids in Billie Jean's elementary school all seemed to come from wealthy families. Many of her classmates owned horses, or they spent weekends golfing at country clubs. Some of the kids looked down on Billie Jean and her family. Billie Jean grew shy and withdrew from her classmates.

One way Billie Jean learned to overcome her shyness was by playing sports. On the baseball diamond or the football field, it didn't matter how much money you had. Everyone started out equal.

Billie Jean's parents encouraged her to play sports as much as possible. Every night after supper her father invited all the neighborhood kids over for a sixty-yard dash in front of their house. Although he couldn't buy Billie Jean her own baseball bat, he carved one for her out of a piece of wood.

Before long, Billie Jean was one of the best players on her block in football and basketball, too. One morning as the family was eating breakfast, Billie Jean asked her father what sport she should try next.

"How about golf?" her father replied.

Billie Jean shook her head. No way. Golf was too boring.

"What about swimming?"

Nope, Billie Jean decided. She wanted to do something she could be *great* at.

"I know," her father said. "Tennis!"

Tennis. Hmmmm. Billie Jean had seen some of her classmates heading off to play tennis after school, but she didn't know very much about the game.

"You run a lot and you hit a ball," her father said. "I think you'd like it."

Billie Jean agreed to give tennis a try. First, she signed up for free lessons at her neighborhood park. Next, she had to find a way to buy a racket. Even the cheapest ones cost more than she could afford. And you couldn't just carve one out of an old tree branch like a baseball bat.

Billie Jean started working odd jobs around the neighborhood to raise money for a racket. Eventually she saved up enough change—eight dollars' worth of nickels and dimes collected in an old mason jar—and took it down to the sporting-goods store. There she found the racket of her dreams: a lavender-colored wooden model with matching nylon strings. It was love at first sight.

And so was the game of tennis. After her very first lesson, when her mom came to pick her up, Billie Jean told her: "I'm going to be the number one tennis player in the whole world!"

But first, Billie Jean would have to impress the most powerful man in youth tennis: Perry T. Jones, president of the Southern California Tennis Association.

A demanding man, Jones required all players to live by his rules of neatness and proper behavior. In Jones's world, boys wore shorts, girl wore dresses. He favored boys over girls and preferred rich kids most of all. If your family donated money to his tennis club, he would send you to play in the important tournaments.

One day, as Billie Jean was getting ready to pose for a group photo with the other players, Jones pulled her aside and said:

Billie Jean's mother had sewn her daughter's outfit by hand. When she found out that Billie Jean was out of the picture, she was furious.

"Don't worry about it, Mom," Billie Jean said with confidence. "Someday, he'll be sorry."

Billie Jean continued to work hard and practice. By the time she was fourteen, she had won enough matches to qualify for the Girls' Fifteen-and-Under Championship tournament in Ohio. It was her big chance to travel and see some of the places she had always dreamed of visiting. But first she needed to ask permission from Perry T. Jones.

Jones insisted that Billie Jean win one more match before agreeing to let her go. She would have to defeat Kathy Chabot, a girl she had never beaten before.

Billie Jean got up at 5:30 every morning, and she practiced harder than she had ever practiced before.

On the day of the big match, Billie Jean was ready. She won the match.

Her next obstacle was to pay for the trip. She asked Jones for help but he refused. Billie Jean then turned to a group of local tennis fans, the Long Beach Tennis Patrons, who raised $350 to cover her travel expenses. Surely now Perry T. Jones would let her go. But Jones wouldn't bend so easily.

It wouldn't be "ladylike" for a girl to travel alone, he said, so Billie Jean's mom would have to chaperone. The $350 wasn't enough to buy two plane tickets, so she and her mom rode the train instead. The trip from Southern California to Ohio took three days. When she arrived at the tournament—either tired from traveling or just overwhelmed by her surroundings—Billie Jean didn't play her best. She lost in the quarterfinals.

When the tournament was over, all the other girls headed off for Philadelphia to compete in yet another championship. But Billie Jean couldn't go. It had taken everything she had just to get this far.

Billie Jean had tears in her eyes as the car full of excited tennis players drove away to the airport. In her heart, she knew that a lot of the players were not as good as she was. When the girls had all gone, she turned to her mother with a look of determination.

"This is never going to happen to me again," she vowed. "I'm going next year even if I have to hitchhike."

Billie Jean made good on her pledge. She worked even harder and became so good that sponsors were willing to pay to send her to tournaments around the country.

The very next year, Billie Jean made it to Philadelphia, competing in the Middle States Grass Court Championships. The year after that, she returned and won her first adult tournament title. In 1961, when she was just seventeen, the Long Beach Tennis Patrons helped raise money to send her to London to play in the world's most prestigious tennis tournament: Wimbledon. Billie Jean won the women's doubles title, the first of 39 Grand Slam championships that she would win during her 24-year career.

PEYTON MANNING

Lord of the Dance

Peyton Manning has played quarterback in the National Football League for more than fifteen seasons. He has a reputation as one of the game's greatest players in critical moments. But the most pressure he ever faced didn't come on the football field—it came on the stage. Long before he was a Super Bowl champion, Peyton Manning was his middle school's master of the tango.

If ever anyone was born to play professional football, it was Peyton Manning. His father, Archie Manning, was the starting quarterback for their hometown team, the New Orleans Saints. His older brother, Cooper, was a natural athlete who would grow up to be the star wide receiver on their high school team.

Peyton dreamed of following in the footsteps of his father and big brother. Being an NFL quarterback was his goal. Football was his passion—he didn't seem to care about much else. One time, when he was three, Peyton refused to play with a boy who didn't share his love for the game.

"He plays with trucks," Peyton said disapprovingly. "I play football."

On Saturday afternoons in autumn, Archie Manning would take his sons with him to the Saints' football practices. The boys hung out in the locker room with the players and took hot baths in the team whirlpool.

On Sundays after the Saints' game, the boys would invade the opposing team's locker room to meet the players and ask about offensive strategy. Sometimes they'd pick up discarded athletic tape from the locker room floor and use it to make their own football. They'd go out on the Louisiana Superdome field and throw passes until their dad called them to go home.

As much as Peyton loved the game, football didn't always come easy. His brother Cooper seemed as if he was built to run and catch passes; Peyton was awkward by comparison. He was also terribly accident prone. One time, while riding in the car with his mom, he fell out the door and cut his head on the road. Another time, while lifting weights with his dad, he tripped and fell face first into a rack of barbells.

But no matter what mishap befell him, and no matter how hurt he was, Peyton picked himself up and kept going. Courage was a trait that would help him throughout his NFL career, where tough decisions and bone-crushing tackles are part of the game.

Another important quality a quarterback must have is the ability to handle pressure. Peyton didn't learn that quality only on the football field. He learned it on stage in front of an audience of family, friends, and neighbors. He learned it beneath the hot spotlights, under the spell of the South American dance known as the tango.

When Peyton started eighth grade, he had the choice of taking a computer class or a musical theater class. Determined to save most of his free time—and brainpower—for football, he chose the theater class. After all, he thought, how hard could it be?

A week into the semester, he found out.

"You have to be in the school play," his teacher informed him. "It's a requirement for the class."

Over the next few weeks, Peyton tried so hard to wriggle out of the production. But as the saying goes: the show must go on. In Peyton's case, the show was called "The Boyfriend." He was assigned the part of Miguel, a headstrong bullfighter who performs a show-stopping tango with Lola, played by his classmate Sabra Barnett. Not only would he have to dance, he would also have to dress like a Spanish bullfighter.

Peyton's costume consisted of a red ruffled tuxedo shirt, tight black pants with a yellow cummerbund tied around his waist, and high-top patent leather shoes. He was mortified.

Even worse than his outfit, Peyton learned that the musical would be performed twice—once on Friday night, for the students, and again on Saturday night, for the families of the cast. Peyton would be forced to dance in front of his parents, his older brother Cooper, and his younger brother Eli. And there was nothing on earth that frightened him more than being on stage in front of his brothers!

Peyton faced a difficult decision. He could try to get out of the play—maybe pretend to be sick or fake a sprained ankle on the day of the show. Or he could huddle up with his theater teacher, study the dance moves, and learn how to tango. Peyton knew the choice he had to make.

On the night of the first performance, Peyton took the stage to raucous applause—and a little laughter—and proceeded to delight the crowd with a spirited performance as Miguel. He stomped, he snorted, he wiggled his fingers above his head like a bull's horns. "I went full-speed on that tango," he later said.

The next night, he was back at it all over again, this time for his whole family. "If they'd had an eighth-grade highlight film," said his mom, "Peyton's tango would have made it." In fact, someone in the audience did make a video recording of the show for posterity.

But it was many years before Peyton would allow anyone outside his family to watch the video of his performance. "Don't look for it," he warned anyone hoping to see him dancing as Miguel the bullfighter. "It's deep in the Manning vault, I can assure you."

And there it remained until one day the footage popped up on YouTube. No one is quite sure how it got there. Maybe one of Peyton's brothers decided to have a little fun at his expense.

By that time, he had already become an All-Pro NFL quarterback, famous for coming through in the clutch—at critical moments—as huge crowds screamed and cheered from the stands. A silly little video wasn't going to bother him.

At a press conference before his first Super Bowl in 2007, Peyton was asked if the upcoming game was the most pressure he had ever faced. Not even close, was his reply. Dancing the tango in front of family and friends was much tougher. "Now that's pressure," he said.

The next day, Peyton went out and led his team, the Indianapolis Colts, to a victory over the Chicago Bears to win the world championship. "It was a wonderful team game," he said afterward. "Everyone did their job."

He may have been talking about the Super Bowl, but Peyton could have said the same thing about his middle school musical.

DANICA PATRICK

The Girl without Fear

It takes a special kind of courage to race around a track in a car going 200 miles per hour. Danica Patrick wasn't born with that kind of courage. She developed it as a kid, competing against boys twice her size on the go-kart tracks of her hometown. The lessons she learned there—about conquering your fears and controlling your emotions—took her all the way to the Indianapolis 500 and beyond.

Today she's known for her fearlessness on the racetrack, but there was a time when Danica Patrick was afraid of almost everything.

She was afraid of bugs.

She was afraid of the ocean.

She was afraid of the dark.

Like a lot of people, Danica was also scared of heights. She managed to conquer that fear with help from her younger sister Brooke. Together they used to climb into the high ceiling that overlooked the factory their parents owned. From there they would gaze down at their mom and dad working below. When they grew bored, the girls would retreat into their parents' office and pretend to be secretaries.

For a while, Danica thought that's what she wanted to be when she grew up: a secretary. But then one day she found her real calling—and that job was maybe the scariest one of all.

It happened when Danica was nine. She and Brooke were playing outside and saw one of her sister's friends drive by in a go-kart—an open-wheel vehicle with a small engine built out of lawnmower parts.

"Maybe that's something I could do," Danica thought as she watched Brooke's friend motor away.

Around that time, Danica's parents were looking for a way for the family to spend time together. Danica and Brooke had a great idea: buy go-karts!

That idea was fine with Danica's parents—both T.J. and Beverly Patrick were racers. T.J. used to race snowmobiles for a living, and Beverly had worked as a snowmobile mechanic. Their first date had even been at a snowmobile race.

When the Patricks found out their daughter also had the "need for speed," they were thrilled. Danica's dad arranged some bottles and cans in a circle to form a makeshift track in the parking lot of their factory. On her first lap around, Danica lost control of her brakes and spun out.

Her kart flipped over and her jacket caught on fire after coming into contact with the hot muffler. Luckily, her dad was able to pull her clear of the wreck. Danica was bruised but otherwise unharmed. Most amazing of all—she wasn't scared! In fact, her first thought was, "Can we fix the go-kart so I can do it again?"

After that, Danica was hooked on racing. She loved steering around tight corners and barreling down straightaways. When she was eleven, she joined the World Karting Association, which sponsors races for young go-kart drivers. Danica's father began taking her to races, which she often won against the all-boy competition.

Being the only girl driver was not easy for Danica. A lot of the boys didn't want to race against her because they were afraid of losing to a girl. Sometimes they'd tease Danica to get her riled up.

But few of these comments bothered Danica. If anything, the taunts just made her more determined to beat the boys at their own game.

Shortly after she started racing competitively, Danica earned her first win. She was lagging behind two other drivers when they crashed into each other and spun off the course. With quick thinking, Danica steered around the collision and zoomed her way to the finish line in first place.

After that taste of victory, Danica drove faster with each race. Soon she was breaking records across the Midwest. She went two years without a single accident. Then she had a big one. Danica was leading a race with one lap to go when two other drivers passed her. Danica sped to catch up as the three drivers approached the final turn. They formed a "V" heading for the finish line. It was anybody's race.

Danica pressed hard on the throttle to pass, but she ended up running over the rear tire of another driver's kart. Her kart flipped over and landed on top of his.

Danica wasn't hurt, but she lost the race. That didn't stop her, though. She strapped on her helmet and got ready for the next competition.

Being fearless gave Danica an advantage over other drivers. But it sometimes prodded her into taking some unnecessary risks. Once, an adult driver cut her off during a practice run. Danica confronted him. She wagged her finger in his face, shouting, "Didn't you see me coming? Look where you're going next time!" That was fearless, but it was also foolish—and rude.

Danica also developed a fierce rivalry with another driver, a boy named Brian. During a race, as they approached the final turn, Danica deliberately crashed into him and knocked his kart off the track.

Her irresponsible behavior upset her father, who made Danica apologize to Brian after the race.

In time, with the help of her dad, Danica learned to control her temper and be fearless without being foolish.

In 1994, when she was twelve, Danica won her first Grand National Championship. She won again in 1996, finishing first in 38 out of 49 races.

When Danica turned sixteen, she was invited to join a road-racing team in England. Instead of go-karts, she would drive real race cars. Though it meant moving far from home, Danica knew this was an opportunity she couldn't pass up.

In England, Danica continued to face her fears. She was homesick and often felt like an outsider. She was one of the only girls on the English racing circuit, and few other drivers would talk to her. Some mechanics refused to work on her car because they thought she couldn't win against the boys.

In her first racing season in England, Danica finished in ninth place. But fear of failure couldn't keep her down. She worked hard and improved her standing year after year. By her third season, she was named the top up-and-coming road-race driver in the world.

Danica's determination attracted the attention of Bobby Rahal, an American racing team leader. When Danica was nineteen, Rahal signed her to his Formula One racing team. She returned to America ready to take on the "big boys" on the Indy car circuit. In 2005, Danica stunned the world by finishing fourth at the Indianapolis 500—the best finish ever by a female driver.

When asked why he signed Danica, Rahal cited her courage in the face of stiff competition: "That she was willing to compete there and endure all of the challenges of racing under those circumstances showed me that Danica was very certain about what she wanted and would stop at nothing to achieve it."

Danica put it this way: "I enjoy a challenge. I enjoy setting a goal and achieving it. It's just a matter of how long it's gonna take."

Part

TWO

Family Matters

BROTHERS,
SISTERS,
PARENTS,
RELATIVES—

ALL OF THESE

Kid Athletes

HAD AN IMPORTANT
FAMILY MEMBER
ON THEIR SIDE.

BOBBY ORR

Little Kid, Big Heart

Even though he became a National Hockey League All-Star, Bobby Orr was rarely the biggest player on the ice. But he never let his small size stop him from competing at the highest level. Raised by his parents to appreciate the importance of hard work, the high-scoring "Number Four" made beating his opponents his number one job.

In wintertime, the temperature in Ontario sometimes drops to forty degrees below zero. Ice on the Seguin River can measure three feet deep.

A Canadian town about 150 miles north of Toronto, Parry Sound in the 1950s was home to about 6,000 people—nearly all of them fans of ice hockey. When the river froze, kids like Bobby Orr would play the sport using sticks made from freshly cut saplings.

As a boy, Bobby developed a reputation as one of the quickest, toughest, and most talented hockey players in town. But he didn't start out that way. When his father first strapped a pair of ice skates onto his son's feet, four-year-old Bobby promptly fell onto the ice.

Bobby's new skates were a set of hand-me-downs from his older brother. They were several sizes too big, or his feet may have been several sizes too small. Either way, Bobby stuffed the skates with paper so they'd fit snugly. It wasn't until he was fourteen that he finally got a new pair of his very own.

But the size of the skates didn't matter. From the moment he first took to the ice, Bobby was crazy about hockey. When it wasn't safe to skate on the Seguin River, Bobby spent his free time firing pucks against the granite wall in his family's garage. In the summertime, he played street hockey with his friends.

Bobby was smaller than most kids in his neighborhood, and the bigger kids would always try to take advantage of him during hockey games. But what Bobby lacked in stature, he made up for in strength and speed. Soon he'd learned to wrestle his opponents and pin them to the ice using a maneuver he called the Parry Sound Flop.

As it turns out, there are many ways to defeat an opponent. On the ice or off, the biggest kids don't always win. Another important way to best the competition is just to work harder.

Bobby knew plenty about hard work from his parents. Both of them worked multiple jobs to make ends meet. Arva Orr, Bobby's mother, was a waitress in a coffee shop and worked in a grocery store. Doug Orr, Bobby's father, drove a cab, tended bar, sold beer for a brewery, and loaded crates at a dynamite factory.

The Orrs encouraged Bobby to work, too. When he wasn't in school or playing hockey with friends, he was doing odd jobs. For a while, he worked as a salesman at a local men's clothing store. One summer, he baled hay for a local farmer, but quickly realized that farm life was not for him.

For another job, Bobby crawled through mud to catch dew worms, which he then sold to fishermen to use as bait.

One of Bobby's most promising jobs was helping in his uncle's butcher shop. His uncle paid him in cash and all the steak he could eat. Bobby loved working there until one day, while he was slicing bacon, he almost cut off the knuckle of his left thumb. That was the end of his career as a butcher.

Bobby even found a job where being short was an advantage. The janitor at his elementary school hired him to help clean classrooms during holiday breaks. And so every day, Bobby scrubbed, swept, and polished the floors. When the furnace needed cleaning, Bobby volunteered to crawl inside and sweep it out. He was the only person small enough to do the job.

But other times, Bobby's size wasn't such an asset. One summer, he worked as a bellhop at a fancy hotel called the Belvedere. Unfortunately, the guests didn't think he was strong enough to carry their bags up to their rooms. But that was his job! When the hotel manager, Mr. Peoples, saw Bobby escorting guests through the lobby empty-handed, he yelled at him.

Bobby didn't want to get fired, so after the incident with his boss he refused to take no for an answer. He had to beg the customers to let him haul their luggage into the hotel. More than once, he was forced to yank suitcases out of a reluctant guest's hands so that he could bring it up to the room.

As he got older, Bobby's passion for hockey grew while his patience for working odd jobs began to wane. He began spending more time on the ice, polishing his game, and less time inside polishing floors. Luckily for him and his family, all his practice and hard work were about to pay off—and in a big way.

The payoff came when he was only fourteen years old. At that young age, Bobby signed a contract with the Boston Bruins, a national hockey team in the United States. The team's managers paid him $2,800 and arranged for him to begin playing for their junior league hockey team in Oshawa, Ontario. He would earn $10 a week.

At first, Bobby's parents did not like the idea of their son moving away from home—he was barely just a teenager. But they couldn't deny him a chance to make it to the National Hockey League.

Bobby's mother agreed to let him play if he agreed to commute to Oshawa for the first year. And so, every Friday after school, friends picked Bobby up and drove him two and a half hours each way so he could play in games on the weekends before returning home for school on Monday morning.

It was a grueling schedule, and it took a toll on the young student. Most people need at least eight hours of sleep every night, and Bobby wasn't getting enough rest. So he slept whenever and wherever he had the chance.

On the professional team, Bobby once again found himself the smallest player on the ice. He weighed just 127 pounds and was competing against older players who weighed as much as eighty pounds more than he did.

Yet somehow Bobby found a way to outplay, outthink, and outfox them all. In his first year in Oshawa, he made the all-league second team. The next year, he was unanimously voted to the all-league first team. At the age of sixteen, Bobby was featured on the cover of *Maclean's*, the national magazine of Canada.

By the time he turned eighteen, Bobby was ready to move up to the big leagues. And though he would never be the biggest player in the NHL, he did have the biggest contract. In 1966, Bobby signed with the Bruins for $50,000 for two years, plus a $25,000 bonus.

All of Bobby's hard work had finally paid off. But with his newfound riches came great responsibility. Bobby was charged with leading the Bruins to a Stanley Cup championship, which they hadn't won in over twenty-five years.

Bobby accomplished the goal in only his fourth season in the league, and he won the most valuable player award, too. Bobby would go on to win three MVP awards and two Stanley Cup trophies. When he retired in 1978, he was widely considered the greatest defenseman in NHL history.

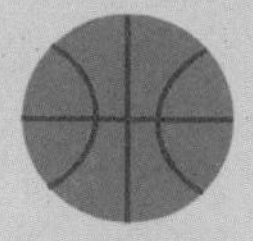

MICHAEL JORDAN

AND HIS

Two Towering Rivals

He grew up to be one of the greatest athletes of all time. But as a kid, Michael Jordan was short, uncoordinated, and prone to accidents. It wasn't until he rose to a challenge laid down by his older brother and his childhood friend that he found the competitive fire that fueled his Hall of Fame NBA career.

Before he took to the basketball court in his signature sneakers, Michael Jordan got into some hair-raising situations. Whether dealing with electricity or angry insects, "Air Jordan" acted more like "Err Jordan."

Once when he was a baby, he fell out of his crib and got stuck between the crib and the wall. At age two, he grabbed the end of an electric wire before his father could stop him. The shock knocked him backward three feet. Toddler Michael was left dazed but otherwise unharmed.

When Michael was four, his cousin handed him an axe and offered to pay him a dollar to chop off his own toe. Michael agreed, but then thought better of the idea. To save face, he tried to whack off just the tip, but he couldn't even do that right. The tip remained attached to his toe, and Michael hopped home crying for his mother.

Bad luck seemed to follow Michael wherever he went. One day, he disturbed a nest of angry wasps under his grandfather's wagon. Another time, while holding an old wooden block as a baseball bat, Michael accidentally swatted his sister in the head. He didn't know the wood had a nail in it, but luckily his sister wasn't hurt.

It didn't help that Michael liked to be a daredevil. He once piled up a huge stack of lawn chairs in his backyard, then jumped off the top of the tower to prove he could fly. He quickly learned that he really couldn't fly and crashed to the ground. Fortunately, the only injury he suffered was a long cut in his arm.

Being accident prone made Michael stand out among his four brothers and sisters. But not always for good reasons.

Michael's father, James Jordan, was embarrassed by his youngest son's lack of mechanical prowess—especially compared to his oldest son, Larry, who loved to help out around the house. "Pops," as Michael called his dad, could fix almost anything.

"Give me a wrench," Pops would say to Michael as he struggled to loosen a gasket underneath the hood of a car. Michael didn't know what a wrench was. Or a gasket, for that matter.

Michael needed to find a way to stand out that didn't involve falling down or accidentally shocking himself. He needed to prove to Pops that he could be the best at something. Or at least be better than Larry.

One day, when Michael was about thirteen years old, Pops built a basketball court in the backyard. He knew how much Larry loved the game, and deep down he hoped Michael might learn to play, too. "This is it," Michael thought. "This is how I finally beat Larry and show Pops how good I can be."

The brothers dubbed their new court "The Rack" and scheduled their first game of one-on-one. For the next year and a half, they played nearly every day after school. The contests were epic—and unfortunately for Michael, the outcome was always the same.

Larry used his superior strength to his advantage. He outmuscled Michael under the hoop—repeatedly dunking on him until his younger brother became frustrated and lost his cool. Sometimes the games would end with brother-on-brother brawls that their mother, Deloris Jordan, had to break up.

As time went on, however, the tables began to turn. Michael grew bigger and stronger while Larry remained the same size.

But despite his growth spurts, Michael struggled. He needed something more to truly grow. It was only after he learned to control his emotions on the court that he was able to use his height to beat Larry to the basket. Larry still won most of the games, but it became harder for him to fend off his brother's drives to the hoop.

One day, Michael dunked on Larry for the first time ever. Finally! Now he had something to brag about at the dinner table.

Still, Pops continued to favor Larry. One time, after a pee-wee league game in which Michael scored the winning lay-up, Pops spent the whole ride home praising Larry for his defense. Michael felt discouraged. If winning the game wasn't enough, what else could he do to convince his father that he was every bit as good as—if not better than—his big brother?

As it turned out, all Michael had to do was grow. In middle school, his growth spurts continued; in a single year, he shot up four inches. Meanwhile, Larry stayed the same size. Eventually, Michael, who was once considered the "runt"—the littlest member of the family—became the tallest kid in his house. He towered over Larry and no longer had to worry about beating his "big" brother on the basketball court.

Soon, even Pops had to admit that the Jordan family had a new sports superstar. Michael was the star pitcher on his baseball team, hurling several no-hitters and bringing the club within one game of the Little League World Series. He was even better on the basketball court. In fact, he was so good that he seemed like a sure thing to make the varsity team at Emsley A. Laney High. Or so he thought.

Fate intervened in the form of a boy named Harvest Leroy Smith, an old friend of Michael's from grade school. Leroy, as he was known, was six feet seven inches tall, nearly a foot taller than Michael. And he, too, was competing for the last spot on the school's varsity basketball team.

On the day the final cuts were posted, Michael and Leroy raced each other to the school's gym. The two boys scanned the list of kids who'd made the team. Leroy looked under "S" for Smith and found his name. Michael looked under "J" for Jordan and discovered the disappointing news: he wasn't on the list.

Sometimes it takes adversity to push a person to do even better. Michael realized that he would have to prove himself all over again. About losing a spot on the team to Leroy, Michael said later that it "was a lesson to me to dig within myself."

With his competitive fire stoked by the setback, Michael joined the junior varsity basketball team, where he averaged 30 points a game. The next year, he made the varsity team. He went on to star on the team at the University of North Carolina and then as a professional with the Chicago Bulls. He won six NBA championships and five most valuable player awards over a career that spanned fifteen seasons. He was so famous, there was even a special basketball sneaker named in his honor: the Air Jordan.

As an NBA player, Michael was contantly measuring himself against the best players the league had to offer: legends like Magic Johnson, Larry Bird, and Dominique Wilkins. But he never forgot the two kids who had set the example for him—his brother Larry and his friend Leroy—even though neither of them ever played a game in the NBA.

Michael and Leroy remained good friends. Throughout his career, whenever Michael checked into a hotel, he signed in as "Leroy Smith" in tribute to his old rival.

And Michael never gave up his rivalry with Larry, either. He often told reporters: "When you see me play, you see Larry play."

One time, the two brothers got together for a friendly game of one-on-one for old time's sake. As they were about to square off, Michael looked down at Larry's feet and said, “Just remember whose name is on your shoes.” Then he blew past him for a dunk.

It was just a little reminder: no matter how good you are or how big you grow, you always need someone bigger, and better, pushing you to be the best.

TIGER WOODS

★ *Kid Superstar* ★

How do you become the world's greatest golfer? Practice, practice, practice. With the help of his parents, Tiger Woods took his natural talent for hitting a little ball into a tiny hole and developed it until he was the best anyone had ever seen. That's how he got to be a worldwide sensation when he was just a kid—and then went on to become the youngest golf champion ever.

"Ladies and gentlemen, I want you to meet Tiger Woods and his father, Earl!"

With those words, the life of two-year-old Eldrick "Tiger" Woods changed forever. As he toddled onto the television stage, Tiger tried hard to focus on the one thing he was there to do: tap a golf ball into a hole. It was a trick he had practiced back home in the garage with his dad. Now he just had to do it in front of a nationwide TV audience. Gulp.

The show's host, Mike Douglas, guided Tiger to the proper spot on the stage. Earl Woods whispered words of encouragement in his son's ear. But when it came time to sink his putt, Tiger was overcome by jitters. He struck the ball, but it sailed wide of the hole. Lucky for him, the host decided to give him a second shot.

This time, Tiger didn't take any chances: he bent down, picked up the ball, and moved it to the very edge of the hole, where he could easily tap it in. The audience erupted into applause. A star was born.

Even at that young age, Tiger was really good at playing golf—so good that one day, almost the whole world would know him by his first name alone.

Tiger's real first name—Eldrick—was made up by his mom. The first letter was for her husband, Earl, a retired U.S. Army officer; the last letter was for her own first name, Kultida. But almost from the beginning, they called their baby boy Tiger, in honor of

Tiger Phong, a South Vietnamese colonel who had saved Earl's life on the battlefield.

After Earl Woods left the military, he moved to Southern California and took up golf. What started out as a hobby quickly became his passion.

When Tiger was a baby, Earl moved his son's high chair into the garage so he could keep an eye on him while practicing his swing. In place of a rattle, he gave Tiger a little putter that he'd made out of a sawed-off golf club.

Over and over, Tiger's dad swatted balls off an Astroturf mat and into a soccer net strung across the garage floor. Looking on, Tiger grew mesmerized by the graceful, repetitive motion. One day, he climbed down from his high chair, waddled over to the mat, and placed his own ball down on the tee. Then he lined up his tiny club and executed a perfect imitation of Earl's swing. He launched the ball right into the center of the net.

A baby hitting a golf ball? It was like nothing Earl had ever seen before. He called his wife to watch their son's amazing feat.

Earl started playing golf with Tiger every day. When Tiger was only a year and a half old, he took him to the local driving range, where they hit buckets of balls into the nets together. When Tiger was three, Earl took him to a golf course near their house. Tiger played nine holes and shot a 48, well over par for the course but still impressive for a toddler.

Soon, the family's living room became Tiger's putting green. After all, it was already filled with obstacles and traps: the coffee table, the fireplace, plants. Tiger had to learn to chip the ball well to get it over the lamp and into the "hole," which was made out of a cup. Practicing in this space would later help Tiger on a real golf course.

Not only could Tiger play golf, he also knew everything about the game without ever having a real lesson. When Earl and Tiger watched golf on TV, Tiger could point out the weaknesses of the professional players. "Look Daddy," he would say, "that man has a reverse pivot!" He instinctively understood the techniques and skills needed to be a superior golfer.

When other kids were drawing race cars and robots in their notebooks, Tiger was sketching himself launching high-arcing moon shots off a golf tee.

Tiger's parents talked together and decided they needed to do everything possible to encourage Tiger to develop his extraordinary talent. Earl Woods would handle golf instruction and training, while Kultida was in charge of motivation and discipline.

Even people with superior talents have weaknesses, of course, and right away Tiger's dad could see that his son had a bad habit of losing focus. So he decided to teach him how to deal with distractions. "I'm a tree," he'd say, and then stand directly in front of Tiger, making him shoot the ball over his head. Another time, just as Tiger was about to make a putt, Earl started jingling coins in his pants pocket. Often times he would cough loudly, sing, or roll a ball into Tiger's line of vision. He'd do anything to break Tiger's concentration.

On and on it went. The distractions angered Tiger, but in time he learned to concentrate fully and sink his putts no matter what was going on around him.

After the *Mike Douglas Show* appearance, the whole world knew about Tiger Woods, the little golf superstar. When he was five years old, Tiger was invited on another national television show, called *That's Incredible!* This time he used his golf club to hit Wiffle balls into the audience, and again the crowd loved it.

All the attention could easily have gone to Tiger's head. But Earl Woods always made sure his son kept his accomplishments in perspective. When another child guest on *That's Incredible!* showed off her weightlifting prowess by picking up all three of the show's hosts at once, Earl pulled Tiger aside.

"Can you do that?" he asked.

"No," Tiger replied.

"That's right," said Tiger's father. "She's special in weightlifting and you're special in golf. There are a lot of special people in the world, and you're just one of them."

After the show, a group of adults approached Tiger and asked for his autograph. Tiger didn't know what to do. He'd never signed his name before, and especially not at the request of grown-ups who wanted a souvenir.

So he just scrawled "TIGER" in large capital letters onto the page.

When Tiger wasn't on the golf course, he didn't feel like a superstar at all. In fact, most of the time he felt like a first-class dork.

One reason for his lack of confidence was a speech impediment. In elementary school, Tiger developed a stuttering problem that other kids would tease him about. His parents took him to speech therapists, but no one could figure out how to correct the problem. Then one day Tiger stopped stuttering on his own. When people asked him how he did it, he said that he had conquered his speech impediment by talking aloud to the family dog.

Faulty vision was another problem for Tiger. From an early age, he was severely nearsighted. He had some trouble in class, unable to read what was written on the board. But only when his blurry eyesight started to affect his golf game did Tiger become concerned.

His parents took him to an optometrist, who prescribed a pair of thick eyeglasses to correct Tiger's vision. Now he could see everything—including how ridiculous he thought he looked.

But in the end, it didn't matter what Tiger looked like or how popular he was in school. He still had that one special talent, and he stayed focused on being the best golfer he could be.

To improve his game, Tiger began competing in local junior golf events near his home in Southern California. When he was eight years old, he entered the Junior World Golf Tournament, a competition for eight-

and nine-year-olds. He needed special permission to play in the tournament, which he won easily.

At age eleven, Tiger beat his father at golf for the first time. And he never lost to him again. At fifteen, he became the youngest player to ever win the U.S. Junior Amateur championship. By the time he graduated from high school in 1994, he had won the tournament three consecutive times.

In 1997, Tiger reached a new high point in his career by winning the most prestigious championship of all—the Masters. *Sports Illustrated* magazine put his photo on the cover: "The New Master," the headline proclaimed. But to his mom and dad, there was nothing new about this master. Tiger had always been their little superstar. Now he was everyone else's, too.

YAO MING

Big Kid in a Small World

At seven feet six inches tall, Yao Ming is one of the world's tallest men. After several years playing basketball in his native China, he spent eight seasons in the NBA and became one of the most famous international athletes of all time. While his immense height may have eased his rise to greatness in some ways, it also put some pretty big obstacles in his path. Being high up always has a downside.

Yao Ming always wanted to be famous. When he was a kid, he dreamed of one day becoming a scientist, an army general, or a politician. But he was destined for bigger things—in more ways than one.

If Yao needed a clue about what he would do when he grew up, all he had to do was look at his parents. His mom and dad were considered the tallest couple in China. Yao's father, Yao Zhiyuan, was six feet seven inches tall and played professional basketball. His mother, Fang Fengdi, stood six foot three and played for the Chinese national team. Soon Yao looked like he would outgrow them both. He started out tall and only continued to grow as the years went by.

When Yao was little, his parents sent him to a doctor to find out how tall he would be. The doctor took an X-ray of Yao's hand and told them he would grow to be seven foot three. Yao was excited when he heard the

news. That would make him one of the tallest men in China!

By his fourth birthday, Yao was already over four feet tall and weighed more than sixty pounds. He was taller than the average eight-year-old!

Three years later, he was four feet eleven inches tall. He towered over all his classmates. His teachers told him that he looked like a stork among chickens.

When Yao entered the third grade, he had stretched to five feet seven inches tall—and he hadn't even had a growth spurt yet! At school, everybody called him "Xiao Juren," which means "Little Giant" in Chinese.

Just as predicted, Yao kept on growing. By the sixth grade, he had grown taller than his mother. He surpassed his father's height before he reached the ninth grade.

Being tall posed challenges for Yao and his parents. Because most homes are made for average-size people, the family had to make their home in a special custom-built apartment in Shanghai so they could live comfortably. Its door frames were larger than normal, so they weren't constantly bumping their heads. The doorknobs and counters were placed high up so that they wouldn't have to bend to reach them.

Their beds were especially long, so they could stretch out at night without falling off the mattress. And there were extra-high shower heads in the bathroom, plus a colossal toilet made just for tall people.

The chairs and couches were built as big as thrones. Visitors often felt like little children in their home.

When one of Yao's friends tried to sit in his chair, his feet didn't come close to reaching the ground.

All the family's clothes also had to be made to order. Yao quickly outgrew regular-sized children's clothing and had to wear his father's hand-me-downs. The outfits could be a little...uncomfortable.

Yao could have easily made a list of all the things he did *not* like about being tall. For example, he was often treated like a grown-up even though he was just a kid. While other kids his age rode public buses for free, he had to pay the full adult fare. The man at the barber shop made him pay full price as well. And because he ate twice as much as a typical Chinese boy, food in Yao's house ran out twice as fast.

But there were advantages to being tall, too. Yao could ride his father's bicycle instead of a smaller kid's bike, for example. And he could reach anything he wanted at any time.

Yao could have used his size to take advantage of the other kids at school. But his parents, who knew what it was like to be the tallest person in the group, taught him to be considerate of others. Whenever his class took a bus on a school trip, Yao gave up his seat so that he wouldn't block anyone's view. When it was time to clean the high windows in the classroom, he volunteered.

In fact, Yao had such a gentle nature that his teachers begin to fear that other kids would take advantage of him. One time, that is just what happened. A bully decided to test Yao's mettle by punching him repeatedly in the arm.

When Yao refused to retaliate, the boy went to Yao's parents and accused *him* of being the bully. Because Yao was so much bigger than his tormentor, his parents at first believed the boy's lie. They scolded Yao and ordered him to apologize. Only later did they find out the truth. After that episode, Yao's mother took it upon herself to teach her son the proper ways to stand up for himself without acting like a bully.

Perhaps the best thing about being tall was that eventually it allowed Yao to find his true calling in life: basketball.

That day came when the Harlem Globetrotters arrived in Shanghai to put on an exhibition of trick shots and fancy ball handling. Tickets were hard to come by, but Yao's mom got two seats close to the court.

Yao came away amazed by the American players' abilities and the fun they had playing the game. After that, Yao played basketball every chance he could—something that the Chinese government encouraged kids who were taller than average to do.

But Yao still had a lot of work ahead to improve his game. He especially had trouble shooting accurately. Sometimes his attempts could be downright embarassing. One day, Yao's classmates nominated him to represent them in a free-throw shooting contest. As Yao stepped up to the line, everyone cheered. But Yao's shot barely grazed the net. An air ball!

The crowd fell silent. And to make matters worse, the next boy in line sank his shot underhanded.

Even close to the basket, Yao found it hard to heave the ball into the hoop. He was tall but also skinny as a noodle. Smaller kids pushed him out of the way, and his friends used to joke that his bony arms looked like chopsticks. After one or two trips down the court, Yao often ran out of steam.

When Yao was twelve, his mother took him to meet a famous Chinese basketball coach. The coach took one look at how Yao walked and immediately dismissed him. He told her that Yao would never be good at basketball because his arms were too scrawny and his butt was too big! He simply did not look graceful enough to be a good athlete. It was a very difficult conversation.

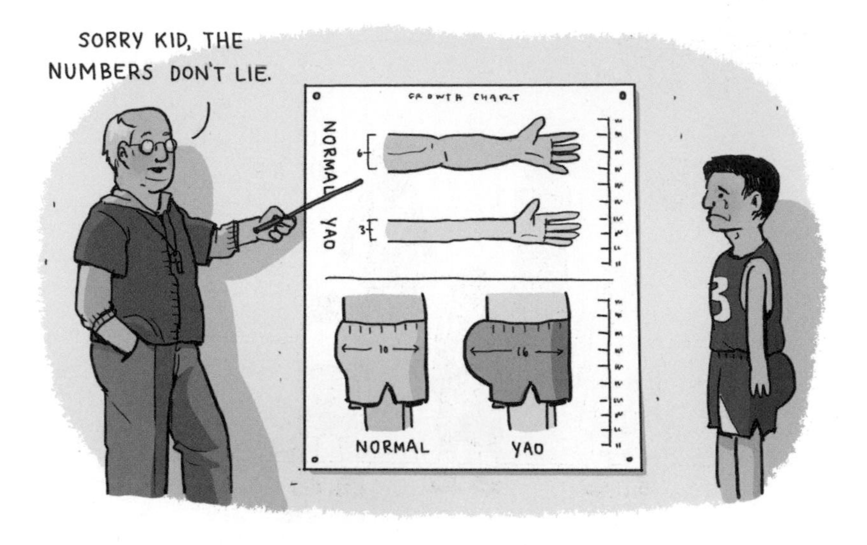

Of course, Yao was discouraged by the coach's assessment, but he didn't let setbacks like these stop him from pursuing his dream. He practiced hard and enrolled in the provincial sports academy. He set his sights on becoming the best young basketball player in China. To build his muscles, he pedaled around the school grounds on a tiny bicycle.

Some of the other students thought he looked funny, but Yao didn't pay attention to them. Slowly but surely, his physical fitness improved—and so did his basketball skills.

When he was thirteen, Yao earned a place on the Shanghai Sharks, a junior league team in the Chinese Basketball Association. He spent four years with the Sharks and then, when he was seventeen, moved up to the senior team. Over the next five years, the Sharks went to the CBA finals three times. In his fifth season, Yao led them to the CBA championship. The skinny kid who had trouble hitting the rim with his free throws was now the most celebrated player in China.

When it came time to make the jump to the United States to play in the NBA, Yao again faced many doubters. Some said he was still too thin and frail to compete with the bigger, stronger American players. A few players even mocked Yao for his Chinese heritage and accent. He might make it to the league because of his size, they thought, but he'd never excel at the professional level in America.

But Yao continued to defy expectations. He made the All-Star team in each of his eight seasons in the league and led the Houston Rockets to the NBA playoffs four times.

Yao Ming's great height had always given him an edge on the competition, but it also took a terrible toll on his body. All those years of running and jumping on hard surfaces led to a series of back, ankle, and knee injuries. Although he still loved playing the game, Yao decided to retire from basketball at the age of thirty to protect his health. No one knew better than he that being tall can be both a blessing and a burden.

GABBY DOUGLAS

Grace under Pressure

Gabrielle "Gabby" Douglas took home a gold medal in 2012 as a member of the "Fierce Five" U.S. gymnastics team at the Olympic Games. But she wasn't born fierce. Though she may have always known how to stand tall on the balance beam, Gabby had to learn how best to stand up for herself when those around her tried to knock her down.

The road to Olympic victory is full of obstacles. To become the first African American gymnast to win an individual all-around gold medal in the international competition, Gabby Douglas had to overcome many challenges—including bullying by some of her own teammates and teachers.

For Gabby (called "Brie" by her family), gymnastics was always easy. Even as a baby, she was already squeezing her tiny hands around the bars of her crib, just as she would one day do with the uneven bars.

At an age when most kids were learning to walk, Gabby was climbing and jumping around. As a toddler, she liked to clamber onto the top of a closet door and then leap off like Supergirl. Couches and chairs were springboards for her airborne adventures.

Sometimes Gabby's daredevil antics attracted unwanted attention. One day, as she was careening through the playground in a toy car, a bully approached and pushed her out of the driver's seat. Luckily for Gabby, her older brother Johnathan was there to help.

It would not be the last time Gabby would have to deal with bullies.

Gabby's childhood became consumed with rolling and tumbling. When she was three, her older sister Arielle taught her how to do a cartwheel. By the very next day, Gabby had moved on to handstands, flips, and other tricky maneuvers. Within a week, she was doing one-handed cartwheels.

Amazed by her sister's progress, Arielle told their mom, Natalie Hawkins, that Gabby should start gymnastics lessons. But Natalie worried that her daughter would hurt herself, and she refused.

Over the next few years, the girls worked hard to wear down their mother's resistance. And although Natalie remained afraid that Gabby might injure herself doing gymastics, she knew that lessons would help her daughter learn to do the movements properly. Without the supervision of a trained adult, who knew what she would jump off next?

So when Gabby was six, Natalie signed her up at a local gym that offered weekend gymnastics classes. Soon Gabby was receiving formal instruction for about six hours a week.

After two years, Gabby was ready to move on to the next level of training. Her mother found another gym that provided more rigorous instruction. The goal there was to train young gymnasts to compete and win tournaments at the highest level, including the Olympics.

At first, Gabby thrived at her new gym. She made friends and learned techniques and strategies from her coaches. But as she improved at gymnastics, Gabby noticed that some of the students began treating her differently. Sometimes she'd see the girls whispering to one another when she entered the locker room. As soon as they saw Gabby, they'd stop talking.

Then, one day, when it was time to clean the chalk off the uneven bars after class, one of Gabby's teammates greeted her with a cruel taunt. "Why doesn't Gabby do it?" the girl asked. "She's our slave." Gabby was terribly hurt by the remark, but she didn't confront the girl or say anything to her instructors. It wasn't until years later that she found the courage to talk about the incident, though she never forgot about it during that time.

Another time, one of Gabby's coaches made fun of her appearance. "She needs a nose job," he joked in front of the other girls. Once again, Gabby gritted her teeth and continued with practice. But when she got home that night—and on many other nights—she cried alone in her room.

Gabby knew she'd been bullied, and she suspected it was because she was the only African American girl in the class. But she was afraid that if she spoke up, she'd be isolated even more—maybe even thrown out of the gymnastics program altogether. So she held her tongue and kept the hurtful comments to herself. She didn't even tell her mother.

Over time, the bullying took a toll on Gabby's performance. She finished in tenth place at her first junior gymnastics competition. At another event, she placed sixteenth and failed to qualify for the U.S. national team. In practices, she butted heads with her coaches. Convinced that she needed to test herself, she begged them to let her try out increasingly difficult routines. But where Gabby sought excellence, her coaches seemed satisfied with mediocrity. One time, after Gabby finished in fourth place at a tournament, her coach was amazed.

"I thought you might be ninth or tenth," he said, "but never fourth!"

Gabby had finally reached her breaking point. How could she have faith in her abilities if her own coach thought so little of her? She knew that it was time to stand up for herself, put an end to the bullying, and find a coach who believed in her.

Luckily for Gabby, she found just such a mentor. Liang Chow had coached U.S. gymnast Shawn Johnson to a gold medal at the 2008 Olympic Games in Beijing, China. He ran his own gymnastics academy in West Des Moines, Iowa.

In the summer of 2010, Coach Chow traveled to Gabby's hometown of Virginia Beach to teach a clinic and look for new talent. On his first day in town, Gabby worked up the nerve to introduce herself and show off some of her skills.

Coach Chow was impressed. He was also friendly and patient, taking the time to show Gabby new moves and expressing confidence in her abilities.

Gabby left the clinic determined to break from her current gym. Now all she had to do was convince her mother to let her go.

"If I'm going to make it to the Olympics, I need better coaching," Gabby told her mom. Natalie Hawkins understood—especially after Gabby revealed details about the bullying she had endured. But the next thing Gabby said threw her for a loop:

Absolutely not, Gabby's mom replied. "There's no way I'm sending my baby across the country."

But Gabby knew she had to take a stand for what she believed in—she had only two short years before the next Olympic Games! Faced with her mother's refusal, all she could feel was frustration and anger. "If I don't change coaches, I'm quitting gymnastics!" she declared, and then she stormed out of the room.

When her anger cooled, Gabby realized that threatening to quit unless she got her way was not a smart idea. Teamwork was the way to go. Once again, she enlisted her sisters Arielle and Joyelle to help convince their mother to change her mind. Finally, after much begging and pleading, they wore her down. Natalie realized that when her youngest daughter set her heart on something, she wouldn't let go. She agreed to let Gabby leave home to pursue her Olympic dream.

In October of 2010, Gabby packed her bags and made the thousand-mile trip from Virginia Beach to West Des Moines. She moved in with a host family and began training with Coach Chow six hours a day, six days a week. Gabby missed her family. There were days during the long, frigid winter when she thought about giving up and returning home to sunny Virginia Beach.

But with the help of her new coach, Gabby consistently improved on each apparatus. She led the U.S. team to a gold medal at the 2011 World Championships in Tokyo and then collected gold, silver, and bronze medals at the U.S. National Championships in 2012.

Later that year, the sixteen-year-old phenomenon—now known affectionately as the "Flying Squirrel"—led the American gymnasts to victory in the team competition at the Olympics. After all the bullying she'd experienced, and all the hard work she'd put in practicing, Gabby had finally found a team with whom she could shine. She was now one of the fabulous "Fierce Five."

Part THREE

Practice Makes Perfect

EVERY

SPORTS LEGEND

agrees on ONE THING:

IT'S IMPOSSIBLE

TO PRACTICE

TOO MUCH.

THESE

Kid Athletes

NEVER

GAVE UP!

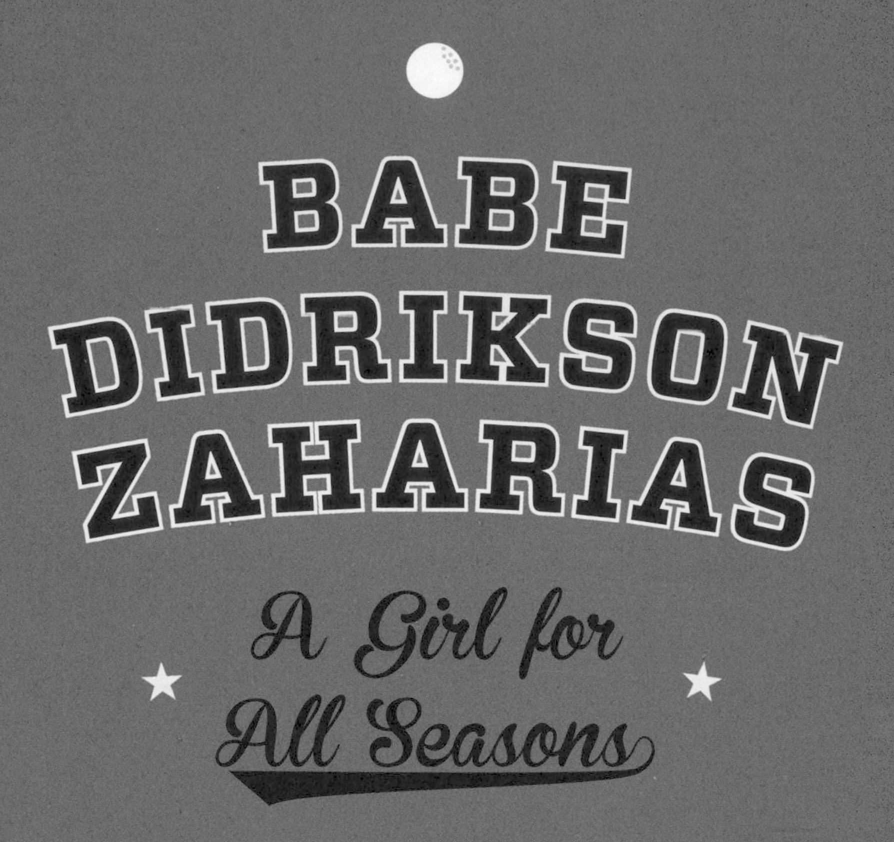

BABE DIDRIKSON ZAHARIAS

A Girl for All Seasons

As a little girl, Babe Didrikson set a goal: "to be the best athlete who ever lived." But she couldn't decide which sport she liked most. So instead, Babe excelled at all of them. She was an All-American basketball player, Olympic gold medalist in track and field, and champion golfer all rolled into one. She might even have become a great circus acrobat—if not for her fear of elephants.

When Babe Didrikson was four years old, a fierce hurricane blew through her hometown of Port Arthur, Texas. Fearsome winds and torrential rain pounded the small Gulf Coast city, uprooting trees and ripping houses from their foundations. While most people hid in their basements, one little girl danced around, laughing in the face of the storm.

After the wild weather had passed, and with water flooding the streets, the girl tried to leap out the second-story window of her home to splash around. But her parents held her back.

Mildred "Babe" Didrikson wasn't afraid of any hurricane. In fact, many of the townspeople of Port Arthur thought she was much like a hurricane herself: fast moving, unpredictable, and impossible to contain.

Babe's father, Ole, knew right away that his youngest daughter was going to be a lot to handle. "No crib I can build is going to hold her," he said when Babe was born.

A furniture maker who had sailed to the United States from his native Norway, Ole settled in Texas with his wife, Hannah, during the state's first big oil boom. But Ole was not an oilman, and he made little money in his newly adopted country. When the storm hit, his family lost most of their belongings, prompting Ole to move inland to a town called Beaumont. It was there that Babe (who later changed the spelling of her last name, adding the surname Zaharias when she got married) would truly leave her mark.

In Beaumont, Babe found a whole new group of townspeople to astound with her fearless, daredevil antics. One day, one of her new neighbors dared her to jump off the roof of her house. She did—and went back the next day and did it again.

In the summertime, Babe was one of the only kids brave enough to swim in the dangerous Neches River near her house. She dodged treacherous rip currents, venomous water moccasins, and snapping alligators. She proved to everyone that she was not afraid.

At school, Babe developed a reputation for pulling pranks and taking risks. One time, she climbed the flagpole and balanced herself on top until the principal ordered her down. Parents warned their children not to follow the example of "that Didriksen girl." But the kids found themselves drawn to Babe just the same.

Maybe it was that Babe acted—and looked—like no girl any of them had ever seen. She hated dolls, wore denim pants, and kept her hair cut short so that it wouldn't get in her eyes while she shot marbles with the neighborhood boys.

As Babe grew older, she started putting more of her energy into sports. She played baseball, football, and basketball; she also liked to jump "hurdles" over her neighbors' hedges. When her father built a jungle gym in their backyard for her brothers, Babe quickly took it over. There was a chin-up bar, a barbell made from an old broomstick with a flatiron at each end, and a trapeze for acrobatic stunts. It was the perfect playset for the daredevil in the family.

For Babe, nearly every activity became another opportunity for play. Once, when her mom asked her to scrub the kitchen floor, Babe strapped a pair of brushes onto her feet and skated around on the soap suds like an ice skater. The way she saw it, chores were just a way to kill time until the next game started.

Even though Babe wasn't taking reckless chances, she still found ways to get into trouble despite herself. One day, her mother sent her to the grocery store to buy ground beef for their suppertime meal. On her way home, Babe spotted some boys playing baseball in the schoolyard.

"This will only take a couple of minutes," thought Babe as she set the package of meat on the grass and ran onto the field to join the game. But the couple of minutes stretched into an hour. By the time Babe returned to retrieve her groceries, a stray dog had eaten all the meat. When her mother found out, Babe was punished for ruining the family's dinner.

By junior high, Babe had developed a reputation as the best athlete in Beaumont. But not everyone shared that opinion. Some boys would not accept that a girl could be better than them at any sport. When Babe was twelve, an older boy named Red Reynolds challenged her on the playground. Red was the star halfback on the football team, and he had heard all about Babe's exploits on the playing field. He was determined to prove that this champion girl athlete wasn't as tough as she seemed.

"Hit me as hard as you can," Red told Babe as he stuck out his chin.

Babe didn't want to hurt Red, but she didn't want to back down either. So she rared back and knocked him down with one punch.

Babe could have been expelled from school for hitting another student, but the principal decided to give her another chance. The principal also made another decision that shocked everybody in town: she issued a decree making Babe the only girl in school allowed to play sports against the boys.

The way was now clear for Babe to achieve her goal: "to be the best athlete who ever lived." She went on to become the star forward on her high school basketball team and made the teams for golf, baseball, tennis, volleyball, and swimming. Then, just when she thought she had mastered every sport, Babe was faced with a new challenge.

Babe was fourteen when a neighbor invited her to join the circus. Minnie Fisher, called Aunt Minnie by the kids in town, was a circus performer. Her specialty was the "iron jaw" act—dangling in the air from a trapeze clenched between her teeth and spinning around like a top.

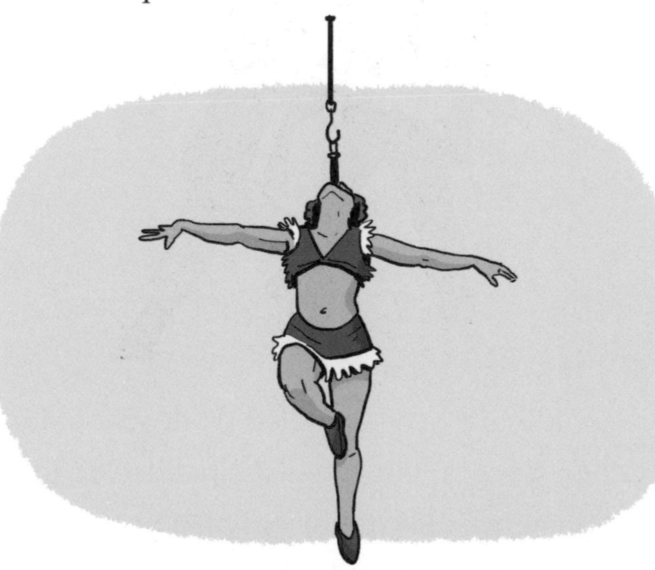

Aunt Minnie had seen Babe practice on her backyard trapeze and thought she had a future on the high wire.

At that time, the circus was one of the only places where a female athlete was allowed to show off her talents alongside men. Babe was tempted by Aunt Minnie's offer and convinced her parents to let her spend the summer under the big top.

Together with her sister Lillie, Babe piled into Aunt Minnie's car for the long drive to California. It was the first time she'd ever been out of East Texas and the first time she'd seen the sights, sounds, and smells of circus life.

Over the summer, Babe learned how to walk across a tightrope, perform flips in midair, and hang by her toes from a trapeze—all to the delight of the crowds. It was an exciting adventure.

Babe was enjoying the new experience of circus life—that is, until the day she was asked to ride on the back of a gray elephant. One look at the giant creature and Babe stopped dead in her tracks.

Walking the tight rope or swinging on a trapeze was one thing, but this animal was huge—and scary. Still, Babe wasn't a quitter, so she stuck with it. After she conquered her fear, Babe decided that, from then on, she would stick to sports and leave the circus acts to the professionals.

As a grown-up, Babe would conquer all the major women's sports of her era, and a few of the minor ones, too. At the 1932 Olympic Games in Los Angeles, she won two gold medals in track and field. A few years later, she took up golf, hitting as many as 1,000 golf balls a day. She ended up winning ten major championships, including three U.S. Women's Open titles.

Nothing pleased Babe more than beating boys at their own games. She once pitched for the St. Louis Cardinals in an exhibition baseball game. She formed her own touring basketball team and later traveled the country playing pool. She even tried to qualify for the men's U.S. Open golf tournament, but she was turned down because she was a woman.

In 1938, when Babe married professional wrestler George Zaharias, the newspapers could barely fit all her accomplishments in the wedding announcement. She was described as a "famed woman athlete, 1932 Olympic Games track and field star, expert basketball player, golfer, javelin thrower, hurdler, high jumper, swimmer, baseball pitcher, football halfback, billiardist, tumbler, boxer, wrestler, fencer, weight lifter, [and] adagio dancer."

When she died in 1956, Babe Didrikson Zaharias was widely considered the greatest female athlete of the twentieth century. Many great sportswomen have followed in her footsteps, but so far none have excelled at as many different sports—or done so with as much panache—as the tenacious tomboy from Port Arthur, Texas.

BRUCE LEE

In the 1960s and 1970s, Bruce Lee did more than anyone to popularize the sport of martial arts. With his powerful roundhouse kicks and lightning-quick "sticky hands," Bruce made fighting look as effortless as walking. But it took many hours of patient study to go from a rambunctious kid on the streets of Hong Kong to an international kung fu superstar.

Bruce Lee was a man of many names. He was born in San Francisco in the year of the dragon, according to the Chinese calendar, and so some people liked to call him "The Little Dragon."

Though he was born in California, he grew up in his family home in Hong Kong. His mother, Grace Lee, named him Jun-Fan, which meant "Return Again," because she believed that one day he would go back to his birthplace. A doctor at the hospital in San Francisco gave him the name Bruce, which is how we know him today.

When he was a kid, Bruce's parents gave him yet another name: Mo Si Tung, or "Never Sits Still." The nickname was perfect because he was constantly in motion. But although Bruce never stopped moving, he didn't really know where he was going. Not until he learned the ancient Chinese martial art of kung fu.

Soon after his birth, Bruce's family returned to Hong Kong. In the crowded and bustling city, they shared a cramped apartment with as many as twenty relatives, several potted plants, and a menagerie of pets—dogs, birds, fish, even a chicken who lived in a cage on the veranda. At times water was scarce, so the bathtub was kept filled from sunup to sundown. Bruce and his family washed themselves behind a curtain.

These surroundings weren't always the most comfortable, especially for an active little boy, so Bruce took to the streets to find room to play.

Sometimes he liked to pretend he was Robin Hood. He and his best friend, Unicorn, would fashion swords out of bamboo stalks, and then they fenced each other for hours. Unicorn was bigger and stronger, but Bruce fought hard and refused to admit defeat.

When he wasn't dueling with the Sheriff of Nottingham, Bruce liked to roam around Hong Kong looking for trouble. More often than not, trouble found *him*. Usually it was because of what he was wearing.

According to an ancient Chinese superstition, there are demons who try to steal male children. To confuse the demons and prevent them from taking their son, Bruce's parents dressed him in girl's clothes for much of his childhood. One night, when Bruce was riding a ferry wearing a girl's outfit, two boys approached and started to make fun of him.

At first, Bruce kept his cool, but as soon as the boat docked, he charged the two boys, kicking one in the shin and sending the other fleeing in terror. Soon kids all over Hong Kong got the message not to mess with Bruce Lee, no matter what he was wearing.

Bruce's other pastime was playing practical jokes. He started out with simple, classic gags, like putting itching powder on clothes. Eventually he moved on to more elaborate pranks. One time he secretly rearranged all the furniture in the family apartment to confuse their cleaning lady. Another time he told his brother to pretend he was on a submarine. When he looked up his jacket sleeve as if it were a periscope, Bruce poured a jug of water down the sleeve, dousing his brother from above.

Preoccupied with pranks and fights, Bruce had no interest in school and often skipped class. Time and again, his teacher would call his parents to find out where their son was.

Exasperated, Bruce's mother made a deal with her son: he could continue to miss classes as long as he told her exactly where he would be at all times. That way, at least she could keep an eye on him.

Still, Bruce's mother worried about his antics. One day she asked him how he expected to make his way in the world.

"I'll become a famous movie star!" was Bruce's reply.

"How do you expect to become a famous movie star?" his mother shot back. "You can't even act like a normal boy!"

But Grace Lee saw glimpses of her son's good qualities among the bad. One time, she noticed Bruce gazing out the window. All of a sudden, he leapt up and ran down to the street. When Grace looked outside, she saw Bruce helping a blind man cross the road.

When he was twelve years old, Bruce enrolled in a new school, La Salle College. While there, he attracted the attention of a kindly teacher named Brother Henry Pang. Brother Henry saw right away that Bruce would be a difficult student. But he also saw that the boy had a good heart, an active mind, and the potential to do great things. He tried to help Bruce channel his restless energy into more constructive pursuits, like running errands, erasing blackboards, and opening classroom windows.

For a time, Bruce gladly did all the chores Brother Henry assigned. But he was still Mo Si Tung and found it impossible to sit and pay attention in class. He again started getting into trouble, joining a schoolyard gang and becoming its leader.

Bruce and his gang were always getting into fights with other kids. Sometimes the police were called. Every day when he came home from school, Bruce would hide under the covers and pretend to be asleep to avoid facing his father's punishment.

Eventually, Bruce was expelled from La Salle College and sent to a different school. He knew then that he needed a better, more positive outlet for his excess energy—and fast.

He found that escape thanks to one of his friends. William Cheung practiced a type of kung fu known as wing chun. Bruce was often on the receiving end of wing chun–style kicks from the kids he occasionally battled, so he decided to master the art of defending himself. He asked his friend where he was training. William introduced him to Yip Man, the local kung fu master. Yip Man agreed to take thirteen-year-old Bruce Lee as his student.

From that day on, Bruce was, in the words of Yip Man's son, "fighting crazy." He took all the energy he used to spend playing pranks and fighting and applied it to studying the finer points of kung fu. Every day after school, Bruce dashed off to Yip Man's classroom for his next lesson. He practiced kicks on the trees he passed along the way. When he went home, he would try out his new moves on the chair next to him at the dinner table.

Bruce became so good, so fast, that some of the older kids in Yip Man's class began complaining that he was beating them too easily.

What was Bruce Lee's secret to mastering martial arts so quickly? It might have been his dance moves. Bruce signed up for dancing lessons around the same time he started learning kung fu. His favorite dance was the cha-cha.

Bruce spent many hours practicing complex routines. He wrote down more than a hundred different dance steps and kept them on a card in his wallet. The superior balance and footwork he learned while in dancing school became part of his kung fu fighting style.

And he kept right on dancing. When he was seventeen, Bruce won the Hong Kong cha-cha championship.

It seemed that Bruce Lee had finally found his calling. But that alone couldn't keep him out of trouble.

Now that he had a reputation as the best kung fu fighter in Hong Kong, Bruce found himself constantly challenged to street fights and rooftop boxing matches. Though he won most of these bouts, they were violent and sometimes bloody. And often they ended with the police being called.

After one such altercation, a police detective arrived and knocked on the door of his family's apartment. Bruce's father answered.

"Your son's behavior has gotten out of control," the officer said. "If he gets into just one more fight, I might have to put him in jail."

That was all Bruce's parents needed to hear. They hoped their son would go to college one day, but now they realized that he had a better chance of ending up behind bars. Bruce's mother urged him to leave Hong Kong and go to San Francisco to live with his older sister. He could stay out of trouble there and pursue his dream of becoming a movie star.

After thinking it over, Bruce agreed that his mother was right. The streets of Hong Kong were no place for a young man with his potential. In April of 1959, he packed his bags and left his home. In his pocket he had only $115, a gift from his parents. Bruce spent the next three weeks crossing the Pacific Ocean on his way to California.

Just as his mother had predicted, little Jun Fan had "returned again" to the city of his birth to seek his fortune. Bruce eventually founded his own martial arts school. Students—including famous actors and outstanding athletes—paid top dollar to learn his distinctive fighting style, which he called "Bruce Lee's Kung Fu."

In time, Bruce's name became so well known that Hollywood producers started calling. He appeared in movies and TV shows throughout the 1960s and 1970s. In one movie, Bruce fought against the celebrated American martial artist Chuck Norris. In another, he squared off against the seven-foot-two-inch basketball star Kareem Abdul-Jabbar. Perhaps his most famous film was his last one, a play on his childhood nickname called *Enter the Dragon.*

All the while, he continued to enter and win martial arts competitions throughout the United States and around the world. When he died in 1973, Bruce Lee was the world's first bona fide kung fu superstar.

MUHAMMAD ALI

AND

The Case of the Missing Bicycle

Long before he took the name Muhammad Ali to reflect his newfound religious faith, a rowdy and rambunctious kid named Cassius Clay displayed all the traits of a great heavyweight champion. He was brash, he was fast on his feet, and he packed a wallop. But it wasn't until he lost his most prized possession that he discovered the real fighter within.

Cassius Clay may not have been born a heavyweight, but even as a kid, he knew how to throw a punch.

At birth, Cassius weighed six pounds, seven ounces—just about average for a baby born in 1942. But like all great boxers, he quickly figured out it's not the size of the man in the fight, but the size of the fight in the man. Or in his case, the infant.

One day when Cassius was six months old, he was lying in bed next to his father, Cassius Sr. He stretched his little arms to yawn and accidentally slugged his dad in the face, almost knocking out his front tooth.

Cassius's dad later called the blow his son's "first knockout punch."

Right then and there, his parents should have known that Cassius was born to box. But just to be sure, he kept giving them hints. He took to walking on his tiptoes, like a fighter dancing nimbly around the ring. And he never stopped talking, as if constantly egging on an opponent. Cassius's mother, Odessa, even started calling him "G. G." for all his "gibber-gabber."

Then there was the peculiar brand of dodgeball that Cassius liked to play. He would challenge his younger brother Rudy to throw rocks at him. With the lightning-fast reflexes he would later show in the boxing ring, Cassius quickly dodged every flying stone.

No matter how many rocks Rudy threw, he was never able to hit his big brother.

Sometimes Cassius's pugnacious disposition got the better of him. For example, he had a bad habit of getting up in the middle of the night and throwing everything in his dresser onto the floor. No one knew why he did it, but his parents counseled him to keep his temper under control.

Cassius and Rudy often got into trouble in their neighborhood in Louisville, Kentucky. One time they destroyed a birdbath in the yard of one of their neighbors, Mrs. Wheatley. People started calling the Clay brothers "the Wrecking Crew" for the damage they caused. Some even started bolting the doors to their houses whenever Cassius and Rudy came around.

That wasn't the kind of reputation Cassius wanted. He realized he would have to find a better outlet for his energy. Fortunately, he was soon presented with the perfect opportunity.

When Cassius was twelve years old, his parents gave him a new bicycle, a red-and-white Schwinn that cost $60. It was just about his most prized possession.

One day he was out riding his new bike with his friend Johnny Willis when a rainstorm overtook them. To stay dry, the boys parked their bikes outside Louisville's Columbia Auditorium and headed inside, where a large bazaar was under way. Cassius and Johnny spent the day browsing the booths and eating ice cream and popcorn.

At the end of the day, when they returned to retrieve their bicycles, the new red Schwinn was gone!

Tears filled Cassius's eyes as he felt his anger rising. What should he do? He had no idea who took his bike, but he did have an idea of what he'd like to do to that person when he found out.

As luck would have it, Cassius found out that a police officer was in the basement of the Columbia Auditorium.

Boiling with rage, Cassius stormed into the basement. But when he opened the door, what he saw was no police station. To his surprise, he discovered a gym filled with men and boys punching bags, jumping rope, and sparring in the center of a velvet-lined boxing ring. If he wanted a fight, it looked like he'd come to the right place.

"Where's the policeman they told me about?" Cassius asked.

Someone pointed to a kindly looking white-haired man who appeared to be in charge of the gym.

"I'm Joe Martin," said the man.

"You're gonna whup him, huh?" Martin replied. "Don't you think you ought to learn how to fight first?"

That thought had never occurred to Cassius. All his life he'd been throwing punches, ducking flying rocks, and promising to pummel anyone who crossed him. He'd never realized that there was a right way and a wrong way to fight.

So when Joe Martin offered him boxing lessons at his gym, Cassius jumped at the chance. The search for the bike thief was put on hold and his training in the ring was begun.

Cassius became a dedicated trainee. He spent almost every waking moment learning to box at the gym. Joe started by teaching him the fundamentals: how to stand, how to punch, how to move his feet. When

Cassius took his turn punching the heavy bag, Martin showed him how to throw rapid-fire jabs instead of big haymakers that would tire him out.

"Cassius, imagine there's a fly on that bag," Martin said.

Almost immediately, Joe saw that his new student possessed one of the most important attributes a boxer can have: speed. Cassius knew how to anticipate an opponent's punch and then dodge out of the way at the last possible second. He never seemed to blink, not even for an instant, always keeping his eyes locked on the hands of his opponent. Cassius was so fast with his eyes, Martin said, that you could hand the other boxer a screen door and he wouldn't hit Cassius with it fifteen times in fifteen rounds.

To complement his quickness, Cassius used fitness and nutrition to build up his body. Some days, he got up at four in the morning and ran several miles before heading over to the gym. For breakfast, he drank a quart of milk and two raw eggs. At school, he needed two trays to carry his huge lunches.

Cassius refused to drink soda pop, because he didn't want to put on weight. Instead, he carried around a bottle of water with a clove of garlic in it. By the time he was done training, he was fit and trim and weighed 89 pounds.

After six weeks of lessons, Cassius was finally ready to step into the ring for the first time. His opponent was named Ronnie O'Keefe. As they squared off under the watchful eye of a referee, the two young boxers looked tiny in their oversized fourteen-ounce boxing gloves.

For three one-minute rounds, Cassius and Ronnie boxed their hearts out. Then they tapped gloves and went back to their neutral corners. Cassius managed to land a few more punches and was awarded a narrow victory. "I will be the greatest of all time!" he proclaimed as the referee raised his arm in triumph. It was the first of many times he would make that claim.

No one knows whether Cassius ever got his bicycle back, but the detour he took the day it was stolen put him on the path to greatness.

Over the next six years, Cassius Clay won 100 of the 108 bouts he fought. By the time he turned fourteen, he was recognized as one of the most promising amateur boxers in America. Just four years later, he was selected to join the U.S. boxing team at the Olympic Games in Rome. He won the gold medal, mesmerizing fans with his lightning footwork and bold, brash personality. He then went on to become one of the greatest heavyweight champions the world has ever known.

His old life as Cassius Clay would soon change, as would his name, when he joined the Nation of Islam. It was then that the legend of Muhammad Ali—forged in a basement of the Columbia Auditorium—truly began.

JESSE KUHAULUA

Don't Mess with Big Daddy

Sumo wrestling is an ancient Japanese sport that combines strength, speed, intelligence, and skill. Most sumo wrestlers are extra large, but it's not uncommon for a smaller man to defeat a much bigger opponent if he uses superior technique. Jesse Kuhaulua, a boy from Hawaii, used both size and skill to rise to the top ranks of a sport that no American had ever conquered.

He started out big—and he just kept getting bigger.

When Jesse Kuhaulua was born, he weighed ten pounds fourteen ounces. He was by far the biggest kid in his hometown of Happy Valley on the Hawaiian island of Maui. At Wailuku Elementary School, his classmates came up with a nickname for him: Big Daddy. They weren't teasing him, though. Everybody liked Jesse. Even the school bullies stayed out of his way, probably because they were afraid to start a fight with him. Nobody wanted to mess with Big Daddy.

Despite its name, Happy Valley was a poor, tough neighborhood. Jesse's family never had much money. Jesse's shoes always had holes. When he wanted to watch TV, he went to the local drugstore to peek at its televion set through the window. But even though he didn't have as much as some kids, Jesse was still happy and active. He liked sports and seemed to have boundless energy for every kind of physical activity.

At the end of a warm day in Happy Valley, Jesse would look up at the stars and dream of traveling to faraway places. Whenever a plane flew by overhead, he imagined he was on board and that it was taking him to Japan—a place he had read about in books. Jesse vowed that he would one day go there to live.

One morning when he was in the second grade, Jesse had a terrible accident that changed his life forever. He was late for school and came sprinting out of his house without looking. As he bounded across the main road, a truck full of pineapples crashed into him—*bam!*—launching him twenty yards into the air. Jesse broke both legs and spent the next six months in a hospital.

After he got out of the hospital, Jesse had to learn to walk all over again. He was in a wheelchair for another four months before he finally took his first steps on his own. When he returned to school, Jesse found it hard to keep up with the other kids because his legs tired easily. He tried out for the softball and track teams, but he was turned down because he was too slow. Jesse thought his days of playing sports were over.

The accident may have slowed Jesse, but it didn't stop his growth spurts. Every day, his mom would give him a quarter to buy lunch at school. And every day, Jesse would pocket the quarter and go without lunch to save some money.

But still he never lost weight. By the time he was twelve, Jesse was six feet one inch tall and weighed 260 pounds. "If I can't be the fastest kid in school," Jesse figured, "I can still be the biggest—and the strongest."

To help his family make ends meet—and to build strength in his legs—Jesse offered to do odd jobs around Happy Valley. He mowed lawns, cleaned yards, and tended the grounds of the local church. Perhaps his toughest job was working for a man who repaired washing machines. Jesse had to carry the machines out of people's homes and load them onto a truck. After a few months of heavy lifting, "Big Daddy" was bigger and stronger than ever.

By the time he got to high school, Jesse had grown another inch and gained another twenty pounds of muscle. He felt so strong that he decided to try out for the football team. This time he made it. He earned a spot in the starting backfield and was soon scoring touchdowns. But when Jesse looked around, he realized he wasn't succeeding because of his athletic ability. The other players were afraid of getting run over by him. As soon as Big Daddy started thundering in their direction, they darted out of the way.

Jesse wished he could find a sport where he could put his skill *and* his size to his advantage.

Jesse's football coach, Larry Shishido, knew just the solution. He told Jesse about the ancient Japanese tradition of sumo wrestling, in which two competitors use a variety of throws, twists, and body drops to try to force each other out of a circular ring. In this sport, size matters. But the biggest man does not always win. Best of all, Coach Shishido said, sumo would help strengthen

Jesse's legs, making him stronger where the accident had left him weakest.

Jesse took to the sumo ring like a duck to water. He joined the Maui Sumo Club and began practicing twice a week.

Soon he was competing in tournaments and bringing home prizes: a transistor radio one time, a bottle of soy sauce another time.

In fact, Jesse won so many matches that he gained a reputation as one of the best *rikishi*—or sumo wrestlers—in Hawaii. When he was seventeen, a group of coaches from Japan came to the islands to watch him wrestle.

"What a monster," said one of the coaches when he first laid eyes on Jesse. "If this boy ever comes to Japan, he will be a champion for sure."

That was all Jesse needed to hear. He had always wanted to travel to Japan, ever since he was a young boy watching airplanes in the night sky. Now it looked like he would get his chance. There was just one small problem: Jesse had promised his mother that he would finish high school first. When the Japanese coaches invited him to Japan to join their sumo stable, Jesse told them they would have to wait another year until he finished his studies.

That was fine, said the Japanese coaches. Instead of being disappointed that Jesse had turned down their invitation, they took it as a sign that he was *majime*, a Japanese word meaning "serious" or "dedicated."

In the meantime, Jesse continued to stay in shape by loading crates onto trucks for the Maui Pineapple Company. Though a pineapple truck had nearly robbed him of his dreams, now it was the agent that kept him strong enough to make those dreams a reality.

At last, when his studies were completed, Jesse won permission from his mother to go to Japan and join a professional sumo stable. It was the beginning of a glorious career. Jesse wrestled in Japan for more than twenty years and was the first American-born sumo wrestler to win a grand sumo tournament.

Now known as Takamiyama Daigoro, the big boy from Happy Valley retired in 1984. He is considered one of the living legends of the sport of sumo.

JULIE KRONE AND THE *Marvelous Mischievous Pony*

To succeed as a thoroughbred jockey, you have to be smart, tough, and strong. Julie Krone is all those things. But she became one of the greatest horse riders in racing history because of one other quality: the special bond she developed as a young girl riding a pony named Filly.

The first time Julie Krone sat on a horse, she knew it was where she was meant to be.

It happened one day when her mother was talking over the sale of one of the family's horses with a neighbor. To show what a gentle animal it was, Judi Krone let her two-year-old daughter climb up on its back. While the adults were talking, the horse began to wander off. Julie instinctively took the reins and began to tug on them, leading the horse back to the stable.

From that day forward, Julie never met a horse she couldn't ride. Until she met Filly.

Filly was the foal of Julie's first pony, Dixie. She was half Arab, half Shetland and just about the stubbornest animal that anyone in Eau Claire, Michigan, had ever seen. She fought against everything. If Julie tied her to a fence, Filly would gnaw through the rope and break free. When Julie tried to put a bridle on her, Filly would plop down on the grass with her legs in the air.

Whenever Julie did manage to mount Filly, the horse bristled and bucked.

More than once, Julie was thrown off and left stranded miles from her house, with no choice but to walk back by herself. She quickly learned that when you're riding a horse, you must be ready for anything.

Julie's mother, worried that no one could control her daughter's horse, wanted to sell Filly. But Julie refused to give up—she worked doubly hard to win the trust of the ornery horse. To calm the animal, Julie placed a T-shirt over Filly's eyes and gently guided her, a training method that usually worked.

But sometimes Julie's techniques backfired. One day when Filly was blindfolded, she charged over a deep hole, narrowly plunging both horse and rider into the gap. Another time, she galloped straight into a barn door. Julie ducked at the last second to avoid banging her head.

Over time, however, Filly learned to trust Julie, and together they faced many obstacles. They learned how to cross crumbling bridges and to ease their way through rushing creeks. Filly learned not to panic when unexpected objects appeared or if obstacles popped up in their path. And Julie provided all the encouragement the horse needed during her training.

Julie's bond with Filly continued to grow and strengthen. She taught the horse to do tricks, like bowing, sitting, and counting with her hooves. She even trained her to answer questions by nodding her head for yes or shaking it to mean no.

Eventually Julie began to enter competitions with Filly. Her bedroom walls were soon festooned with ribbons won at riding and jumping events. People began to say that Julie had a special gift for communicating with horses.

As she grew older, Julie set her sights on a career racing thoroughbred horses. The ribbons on her wall were replaced by photographs of jockeys and racetracks.

When she was eighteen, Julie left home for Kentucky to pursue her dream of becoming a professional jockey. Over the next thirteen years, she won more than three thousand races across America. In 1993, she won the Belmont Stakes astride a horse named Colonial Affair, making her the first female jockey ever to win one of the classic Triple Crown races.

During the time that Julie was away from home winning races, her mother sold Filly to one of their neighbors, who then sold her to a horse farm in another part of Michigan. Though Filly was no longer a part of her family, Julie never stopped thinking about her.

One night, after Julie had been a successful jockey for several years, she began having dreams about her old horse. In her dreams, Julie sensed that Filly was in danger and needed her help.

Not knowing where to find Filly, she drew up a list of every barn in the state of Michigan and began calling around, searching for her friend.

It seemed hopeless, until Julie reached the last barn on her list. The woman on the phone said she now owned Filly, but wouldn't for much longer. She was just about to take the horse to be sold at an auction.

"Don't sell her!" Julie implored. "I want to buy her. I'll be there in two days!"

Hitching a horse trailer to her truck, Julie drove all the way to Michigan from her home in New Jersey.

When she arrived at the barn, Filly's new owner took her out to the field where the horse was tied. At first, Julie didn't recognize her. Filly was now very old.

But once she heard about the animal's ornery disposition, she knew she had the right horse.

"Don't get on her," the farm owner warned. "She'll buck you off. She bucks everybody off."

But Julie knew better. She untied Filly and hopped up on her back. It was just like old times. Filly remembered every trick Julie had taught her.

The owner couldn't believe her eyes. No one had ever been able to ride this crazy horse. She agreed to let Julie buy Filly for $500.

When Julie got home to her farm in New Jersey, she took Filly to a veterinarian and learned that her fears for the horse were well founded. Filly had a hoof disease that could have killed her if it had gone undetected. It took almost a month, but Julie was able to nurse Filly back to health.

When Filly was better, Julie called her best friends, Pete and Paula Freundlich, and asked them to bring their two daughters to meet her old riding companion. When the family arrived, Julie led the girls out to the stall.

"This is Filly," Julie said, "and she's for you."

Julie knew she could no longer care for Filly, but she hoped that the two girls, who were six and four years old, would have the same energy and patience she had once had at their age. From the joyful looks on the girls' faces, Julie knew she had chosen wisely.

Before Filly went to live with her new family, Julie just had a few words of warning:

"Don't be misled by this pony," she said. "She is a

diabolical creature inside, full of spit and nasty thoughts. If you girls can learn to ride Filly, then you'll be able to ride any horse in the world."

When Julie Krone retired from racing, she was inducted into the National Museum of Racing and Hall of Fame. Her long career racing horses had begun on the back of a "rotten little pony" who became her best friend.

LIONEL MESSI

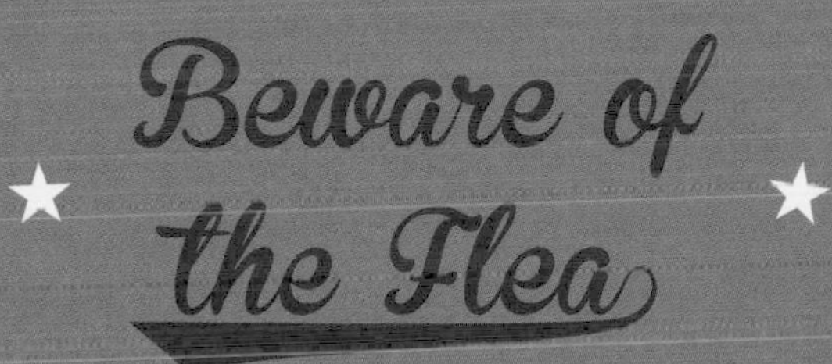

In soccer, being small and fast is usually an advantage. But you have to be tough if you want to take the hits that come with being the shortest player on the field. Though a growth hormone deficency threatened to hold him back, Lionel Messi surged past bigger opponents to become one of the greatest soccer players of his generation.

From the moment Lionel "Leo" Messi took his first steps at just nine months old, he spent all his time chasing soccer balls his older brothers left around the house. But you can't play soccer indoors, so Leo went looking for a new place to get his kicks.

Leo left his house in search of some space. The first time he wandered outside, a bicycle whizzed past and bowled him over.

Shaken up and a little bruised, Leo picked himself up and toddled back inside. That night, as he lay in bed, he noticed that his arm was swollen. His parents took him to the hospital, where a doctor confirmed that he had broken a bone during the accident. Leo's parents were amazed—he had gone the entire day without once complaining about the pain. It was a lesson that Leo's soccer opponents would one day learn: you can knock

Leo Messi down, but you can't stop him.

When Leo turned three, he received his first soccer ball as a birthday present. It was white with a blue five-pointed pattern, just like the kind used by the pros.

"Look after him!" Leo's mother shouted to his brothers as he ventured outdoors to play with the older boys. Leo was one of the smallest kids on his block.

Leo and his soccer ball soon became inseparable—he brought it everywhere. And if he couldn't bring the ball with him, he'd fashion one out of rags, rolled-up bags, or wads of Silly Putty. He even took the ball to bed with him at night, squeezing it between his legs as he drifted off to sleep.

When he couldn't find someone to play soccer with, Leo would kick his ball against a wall in his hometown of Rosario, Argentina. *Bam, bam, bam*—over and over until his neighbors complained. But nothing could stop his practice drills.

Eventually, a soccer coach took notice of Leo's dedication. "There's no way of stopping this boy," the coach said. "He spends all day playing and he wants to play when the sun has gone down. When everybody is asleep!"

Sometimes bullies tried to separate Leo from his soccer ball. They'd grab it and throw him on the ground. But Leo always got back up and went right on dribbling. It almost seemed as if the ball was attached to his foot with string like a yo-yo.

As he grew older, Leo stayed small for his age. But what he lacked in size, he made up for in skill.

On his first day of school, Leo was told he couldn't play soccer because he was too fragile. To prove to his teacher that he was as good and as strong as the other kids, he put on an amazing dribbling exhibition. From then on, he was the first player picked when the kids chose teams for soccer games.

Leo joined a local youth team, and his reputation as Rosario's wee wizard of soccer grew. Kids started calling him "The Maestro" because he was like a brilliant musical conductor when he had the ball. It didn't matter how small he was. No one could take the ball away if he refused to give it up.

Although Leo's stature never bothered him on the soccer pitch, his parents were becoming concerned about his inability to grow. The other kids in town grew an inch or two every year, but Leo stayed the same height.

When Leo was eleven years old, his parents took him to a doctor. After a series of tests, he learned that he had a growth hormone deficiency, or GHD. In other words, he had stopped growing. Leo would need to start treatments if he didn't want to stay stuck at the same height for the rest of his life.

Night after night, before going to sleep, Leo had growth hormone injections in his legs. At first, he was afraid of the needles and asked his mother to give him the shots. But eventually he decided that it was something he needed to learn to do for himself. The first few times he tried, his hand shook. With time and practice, however, he got used to it. He started carrying a little cooler at all times. Inside were the needles for his injections.

The treatments seemed to be working. Leo began to grow. But his parents had trouble paying for the medicine. Leo's soccer club agreed to help, but even they couldn't afford to cover all his medical bills.

Eventually a team in Spain called FC Barcelona came to Leo's rescue. The coaches there had heard about the soccer-playing sensation from Argentina, and they were eager to see him in person. If Leo could only convince them to let him join the team, they would cover the cost of his hormone treatments.

Now Leo had a mission. Using a borrowed video camera, he filmed himself juggling oranges with his feet like they were soccer balls.

He sent the video to the FC Barcelona office in Spain. The team officials were so impressed with Leo's skills that they offered him a tryout.

Leo and his father made the 14-hour journey from Rosario to Buenos Aires, then across the Atlantic Ocean to Barcelona. It was the first time Leo had ever been on an airplane. The turbulence made his stomach churn.

When he arrived, the FC Barcelona coaches looked him over. Some of them were not impressed. They wondered if this was a joke. How could this short little boy compete against the biggest, baddest, best players in Spain? After sizing him up, one of the team officials ruffled Leo's hair. "You better be good," the man said. "Because you're so small."

On his first day of practice, Leo was nearly overcome with nervous jitters. Before he could even get inside the locker room, he froze. He started to change into his soccer uniform right there in the hallway. Eventually, he worked up the courage to go inside and meet his teammates.

"Be careful with him," one player said. "He's very small. Don't break him." Others called him "midget" or "The Flea." These were not compliments. Leo was so afraid the other players would not accept him that he sat off by himself and didn't say hello to anyone.

Once the day's scrimmage began, Leo started to feel more comfortable. Everyone was struggling to reach his level. He stole the ball from the team's best offensive player, then beat its best defensive player in a one-on-one situation. He scored five goals, dazzling the FC Barcelona coaches with his speed and foot skills.

From then on, no one called him names. When they used the word "flea," it was to taunt someone who had just been left in Leo's dust, as in: "You guys just got beat by the Flea!"

The FC Barcelona officials were so impressed by Leo's play that they offered to pay for his hormone treatments and move his entire family to Spain. In fact, they were in such a rush to snatch him up before another team did that they drew up a contract on a paper napkin. Leo and his parents signed it right then and there.

In 2000, Leo's family packed up their home in Argentina and made the journey across the Atlantic. This time, the move would be permanent. Leo had to continue with his growth hormone therapy and kept growing at a normal rate. He would never be tall, but he was more than big enough to match up against the best youth soccer players in the world—which he did every day. He joined Barcelona's under-fourteen team and quickly became its star player.

Leo's opponents occasionally tried to take advantage of his size. In only his second game in Barcelona, he was fouled so hard that he had to leave the field in an ambulance. He had fractured a bone in his face. But Leo returned even more determined to lead his team to victory. "Something deep in my character allows me to take the hits and get on with trying to win," he said.

Undaunted by the rough play, Leo zoomed through the junior ranks and made the regular Barcelona club at age 16. In 2005, he became the youngest player ever to score a goal for the franchise. He went on to lead "Barca" to six league titles in his first ten years with the team. Though he topped out at only five feet seven inches tall, Lionel Messi had become one of the biggest soccer stars in the world.

FURTHER Reading

WANT MORE

STORIES

ABOUT THE

AND YOUR

FAVORITE

SPORTS?

TURN THE PAGE

AND KEEP

READING!

★ BIBLIOGRAPHY ★

There are many great books about great athletes, including autobiographies (books written by the person about himself or herself) and biographies (books about famous people written by someone else). The following is a list of the main sources used by the author in researching and writing this book.

PART ONE

IT'S NOT EASY BEING A KID

Babe Ruth

Brother Gilbert, CFX. *Young Babe Ruth: His Early Life and Baseball Career, from the Memoirs of a Xaverian Brother.* Edited by Harry Rothgerber. Jefferson, NC: McFarland & Co., 1999.

Crawford, Bill. *All American: The Rise and Fall of Jim Thorpe.* Hoboken: John Wiley & Sons, 2005.

Creamer, Robert W. *Babe: The Legend Comes to Life.* New York: Fireside, 1974.

Krull, Kathleen. *Lives of the Athletes: Thrills, Spills (and What the Neighbors Thought).* Illustrated by Kathleen Hewitt. San Diego: Harcourt Brace & Company, 1995.

Montville, Leigh. *The Big Bam: The Life and Times of Babe Ruth.* New York: Broadway Books, 2006.

Wagenheim, Kal. *Babe Ruth: His Life and Legend.* New York: Praeger Publishers, 1974.

Jackie Robinson

Krull, Kathleen. *Lives of the Athletes: Thrills, Spills (and What the Neighbors Thought).* Illustrated by Kathleen Hewitt. San Diego: Harcourt Brace & Company, 1995.

Billie Jean King

Hasday, Judy L. *Extraordinary Women Athletes.* New York: Children's Press, 2000.

King, Billie Jean. *Billie Jean.* With Kim Chapin. New York: Harper & Row, 1974.

———. *Billie Jean.* With Frank Deford. New York: Viking Press, 1982.

Peyton Manning

Christopher, Matt. *On the Field with . . . Peyton and Eli Manning.* Text by Stephanie True Peters. New York: Little, Brown, 2008.

Manning, Archie, and Peyton Manning. *Manning: A Father, His Sons, and a Football Legacy.* With John Underwood. New York: HarperCollins, 2000.

Danica Patrick

Patrick, Danica. *Danica: Crossing the Line.* With Laura Morton. New York: Simon & Schuster, 2006.

PART TWO

FAMILY MATTERS

Bobby Orr

Brunt, Stephen. *Searching for Bobby Orr.* Toronto: Seal Books, 2007.

Orr, Bobby. *Orr: My Story.* New York: G. P. Putnam's Sons, 2013.

Michael Jordan

Halberstam, David. *Playing for Keeps: Michael Jordan and the World He Made.* New York: Broadway Books, 2000.

Krugel, Mitchell. *Jordan: The Man, His Words, His Life.* New York: St. Martin's Press, 1994.

Tiger Woods

Helling, Steve. *Tiger: The Real Story.* Cambridge: Da Capo, 2010.

Yao Ming

Larmer, Brook. *Operation Yao Ming: The Chinese Sports Empire, American Big Business, and the Making of an NBA Superstar.* New York: Gotham Books, 2005.

Ming, Yao. *Yao: A Life in Two Worlds.* With Ric Bucher. New York: Hyperion, 2004.

Gabrielle Douglas

Douglas, Gabrielle. *Raising the Bar.* Grand Rapids, MI: Zondervan, 2013.

PRACTICE MAKES PERFECT

Babe Didrikson Zaharias

Hasday, Judy L. *Extraordinary Women Athletes.* New York: Children's Press, 2000.

Krull, Kathleen. *Lives of the Athletes: Thrills, Spills (and What the Neighbors Thought).* Illustrated by Kathleen Hewitt. San Diego: Harcourt Brace & Company, 1995.

Van Natta, Don, Jr. *Wonder Girl: The Magnificent Sporting Life of Babe Didrikson Zaharias.* New York: Little, Brown, 2011.

Wallace, Rich, and Sandra Neil Wallace. *Babe Conquers the World: The Legendary Life of Babe Didrikson Zaharias.* Honesdale, PA: Calkins Creek, 2014.

Bruce Lee

Koestler-Grack, Rachel A. *Bruce Lee.* New York: Chelsea House, 2007.

Krull, Kathleen. *Lives of the Athletes: Thrills, Spills (and What the Neighbors Thought).* Illustrated by Kathleen Hewitt. San Diego: Harcourt Brace & Company, 1995.

Thomas, Bruce. *Bruce Lee: Fighting Spirit.* Berkeley, CA: Blue Snake Books, 1994.

Muhammad Ali

Hauser, Thomas. *Muhammad Ali: His Life and Times.* New York: Touchstone, 1991.

Remnick, David. *King of the World: Muhammad Ali and the Rise of an American Hero.* New York: Vintage Books, 1998.

Jesse Kuhaulua

Adams, Andrew, and Mark Schilling. *Jesse! Sumo Superstar.* Tokyo: Japan Times Ltd., 1985.

Kuhaulua, Jesse. *Takamiyama: The World of Sumo.* New York: Harper & Row, 1973.

Julie Krone

Koda-Callan, Elizabeth. *The Good Luck Pony.* With contribution by Julie Krone. New York: HarperCollins, 1993.

Krone, Julie. *Riding for My Life.* With Nancy Ann Richardson. New York: Little, Brown, 1995.

Lionel Messi

Balague, Guillem. *Messi.* London: Orion Publishing, 2014.

Part, Michael. *The Flea: The Amazing Story of Leo Messi.* Beverly Hills: Sole Books, 2013.

★ INDEX ★

E

F

G

H

I

J

K

L

M

N

O

P

Q

R

S

ACKNOWLEDGMENTS

DAVID STABLER would like to thank Jason Rekulak for drafting the players, Doogie Horner for drawing up the plays, Andie Reid for designing the game plan, Mary Ellen Wilson for sending in the substitutions, and the entire Quirk All-Star team for always giving 110%. Special thanks to Nicole De Jackmo and Kelly Coyle Crivelli for helping to spread the word about our books.

DOOGIE HORNER would like to thank Jason Rekulak for his incredible editing, Mario Zucca for his wonderful coloring, and Andie Reid for her awesome design. Also Mary Ellen Wilson for keeping us on track, and all the other people at Quirk Books for being generally cool. Thanks of course to David Stabler for writing such entertaining stories, and my wife, Jennie, for making coffee in the morning and being so pretty.